MW00326139

LONGING

for

WHOLENESS

To Cheri –

Here's to happy

memories yet

to be –

Love Linda

LONGING

for

WHOLENESS

filling the void in my soul

LINDA LOUISE

Tate Publishing & Enterprises

Longing For Wholeness
Copyright © 2007 by Linda Louise. All rights reserved.

This title is also available as a Tate Out Loud product. Visit www.tatepublishing.com for more information.

No part of this publication may be reproduced, stored in a retrieval system or transmitted in any way by any means, electronic, mechanical, photocopy, recording or otherwise without the prior permission of the author except as provided by USA copyright law.

The opinions expressed by the author are not necessarily those of Tate Publishing, LLC.

Published by Tate Publishing & Enterprises, LLC
127 E. Trade Center Terrace | Mustang, Oklahoma 73064 USA
1.888.361.9473 | www.tatepublishing.com

Tate Publishing is committed to excellence in the publishing industry. The company reflects the philosophy established by the founders, based on Psalms 68:11,
"The Lord gave the word and great was the company of those who published it."

Book design copyright © 2007 by Tate Publishing, LLC. All rights reserved.
Cover design by Elizabeth A. Mason
Interior design by Steven Jeffrey

Published in the United States of America

ISBN: 978-1-60247-515-1
1. Christian Living   2. Practical Life: Personal Growth
07.08.20

DEDICATION

This book is dedicated, beyond what there is love to express, to the life and memory of my brother, James Jay, lovingly known as Jimmy. Without him, I would not be who I am today, and this book would not have been written. May the words of my life touch your life to its depths as his life did mine.

ACKNOWLEDGEMENTS

This writing was accomplished because of the involvement and influence of these people, both in my life and with the book:

Jane–The first audible voice to speak, "Write your story; people need to hear what you have to say." And for the nine years following, frequent encouragement to get this book done, that people need it. A faith warrior to make the way.

Nancy–After reading a few chapters in the beginning, her reaction was, "It gives me hope—there is hope." Her continuous prayer and intercession to finish the work, make it complete and get it out there for others. Another prayer warrior.

Mary Lou–The eagle eye, whose critique in what and how things were written, created a more in-depth and sincere expression so readers can identify with something within their own being. I took my concepts to her for feedback.

Diane–Her professional editorial expertise and skills assisted in fine-tuning this work. She brings to the process a unique insight into the dynamics of relationships, able to identify the voids where things seemed incomplete.

Pat and Jim, Jan and Bob, Bob and June–Spiritual mothers and fathers along this nine-year journey who were enthralled at any little progress, providing support and faith for me to forge out an area of my destiny, the wind beneath my wings.

Lennie–Upon reading bits and pieces of this work over the years she asked, "Gee, Linda, where is the rest so I can finish the story?" Very encouraging.

Shawn–Our friendship helped me see "me" in the totality of who I am, and how valuable I am as a person. He confronted the little boxes I lived in, let me be me, and helped to gel the pieces of my life.

TABLE OF CONTENTS

FOREWARD

This book is about overcoming: fear, rejection, and real betrayal. It's about love and mercy. Linda tells her story with a deep, raw, honesty, and it will touch every heart. We all have these places in our hearts and lives, but most of us never acknowledge them, let alone speak of them.

This book will speak especially to those of us who have known abuse as children, whether sexual, emotional, or physical, and the indelible mark it leaves on our lives.

The experiences Linda speaks of will help us all to examine our own lives with more honesty and courage. This is not a morbid, "poor me" book. It is a story from behind the eyes of a little girl, and Linda has the amazing storytelling ability to take us right there, in the moment.

I loved this book because its healing, redemptive, and forgiving essence ministered deeply to my spirit. I couldn't turn the pages fast enough to see what would happen next.

I am thankful that someone has the courage to open their heart at such a deep level. Somehow, it's personally humbling to my own heart. This is a story of victory, and it's available for all of us through the great, good kindness of our merciful and redeeming heavenly Father.

Sharron Heenan

A forever friend

INTRODUCTION

Whose eyes do you see yourself through? The journey of my life has been the lessons of learning to see myself through the eyes of a heart that loves me, accepts me with no criticism, and wants me to become and express everything I am and can be. It encompassed trials for finding purpose, fulfillment, joy, and peace in the life before me to live. It has been learning to see myself not through the eyes of others, nor even my own with all of the limitations I have as a human, but to see through the eyes of God's heart. Yes, God's heart has eyes and He perceives us through the love, compassion, and caring that only He has. To see ourselves through His love, in all its greatness and all its simplicity, brings a wholeness to living that is almost beyond words to express. It is the wholeness of knowing deep inside of your being that you were created for a good intention and you have the right to live that out to its fullest.

"I pray that the eyes of your heart may be enlightened, so that you may know what is the hope of His calling, what are the riches of the glory of His inheritance in the saints." Ephesians 1:18 NAS

PART ONE

PUTTING IT ALL TOGETHER

"You have no idea what a miracle you are!" The first time I heard these words was in 2004. I was fifty-seven. It was my first visit to see Miriam, a psychologist and counselor. A car accident in 1998 stopped my life—or I should say changed the track my life was on. Two years after the accident, the post-traumatic stress disorder set in. After suffering with it for over three years, my daily life became almost unbearable. The PTSD destroyed any sense of "self" that I had left, just trying to live through each day, one minute at a time, without my body exploding internally with hidden fear and trauma symptoms. I had to learn how to mask and medicate these symptoms so my life could appear normal, so I could keep functioning. The PTSD also turned out to be the final thing that forced me into surfacing the pieces and parts of my life that were like fragments, a thought here, a feeling there, all muddled in with pain, sadness, and not feeling like I belonged anywhere. It stirred up the buried feelings of my whole life. They were churning within me with no resolve, like a tornado—spinning round and round with no way out. I knew I had to find healing from what was within or I would die. I had been ill continually for almost two years with flues, colds, and sinus infections. I felt like I was wearing out.

On my first visit to see Miriam, I mentioned the various

things that happened to me from my childhood, just touching on them lightly. No time yet for details and certainly no fortitude yet on my part to want to speak of them. Miriam sat in the chair opposite me, seemingly restless, moving a hand to her face, then her head, then the other arm, and crossing, then uncrossing and crossing her legs again. I sensed she was trying not to let what she was really thinking show on her face. "You really don't know what a miracle you are. People who have lived what you have just are not here any longer. They don't make it this far in life."

The second session and the ones following all encompassed the same theme: "Stop! Stop! Stop right now! You just don't see yourself right—you have no idea what a miracle you are. Not only the fact that you are still here, but that you have raised two wonderful sons and are holding a good job. You have an inner strength that most people don't have." With great expression, conviction, and emphatic movements, Miriam sometimes would almost yell at me for how I saw myself. I would sit there listening—motionless and emotionless—just looking at her, wondering to myself, *I wonder what she is really trying to say?* I did not react, nor respond, just looked at her. I stayed safe within my learned behavior of showing no emotions, no feelings, and no thoughts. This is a good description of how I lived and viewed my life. My sister and cousin even teased me with the name "Old Ironsides" when I was in the eighth grade.

"You don't know what a miracle you are!" I heard these same words many times over a period of two years as Miriam listened to me, gave me her perspective, and gave me a safe place to let me begin to feel. The most miraculous thing of all was to begin to express how I felt and what I had experienced and to learn that the shame, contempt, and agony I had lived in was not because of me. She said to me several times, "I have seen hundreds of people. And on a scale of one to ten, you're way up there." As she would say this, I thought, *Hmm. I only know my life; I can't compare how I feel inside with how another has experienced living.* What came to my mind when she said this was a time when I was six and was invited to a classmate's birthday party. Margaret was the picture of the perfect little girl. She was very ladylike, very poised and mannerly, straight black hair, perfect pink skin, and always smiley with a calm confident demeanor. I went to Margaret's party after school one night, even wondering why I had been invited. Margaret's mother was there, young and beautiful, and about seven other little girls. What I remember was Margaret's mother calling her "honey," "sweetie," and other endearing names. She brushed the hair from her forehead and looked at her like she was the greatest thing in the whole world. I sat there feeling awkward and out of place, and hating Margaret because of the endearing words and affection shown to her by her mother. I could not consciously—at that time—remember a child, but most especially me, shown such a display of affection. But somewhere in my subconscious, somewhere deep, I had a buried treasure that someone did love me like that once, and cherished me. I just had no conscious awareness until years later as Aunt Jan told me about Uncle Ted, I knew what I felt in my heart for years was true.

After a year and a half of visits with Miriam, I went back to my fortieth year class reunion. This was the first time I had gone back since graduation. I went back because I wanted to face the way I saw myself back then. I wanted to pull another fragment of me into who I am today and find another element of truth. What I found was how my classmates viewed me, in comparison to how I saw myself. The two views were on opposite sides of the spectrum. My classmates saw me as beautiful, very smart, and very, very quiet. Well, the quiet part I knew. I saw myself as not only shy, but disliked and as a failure. Experiencing my classmates with my "new" eyes, I realized it was me that kept them out. People have always looked at the outside of me and thought that I had it made. They did not know or see what was happening inside and how very difficult my life really was, just not only to keep going, but to maintain that façade—so everything would seem okay.

Miriam was not the first counselor that I had gone to. In 1992 I had sessions for a year to work through some of the devastating effects of a bad marriage and divorce. After eight years of being divorced, I had a boyfriend. In bringing someone into my personal life, I realized the behaviors I had acquired over the years were not how I wanted other people to see me living. My boyfriend even drove me to see this counselor weekly. Our discussions were mostly about my ex-husband and my mother. The counselor asked to see a picture of me as a child, so I took her a picture that I was particularly fond of. I was holding onto the tongue of a tiny rusty wagon that was my friend. Mom had sworn at me while she was taking this picture. She had been taking pictures of Jimmy, my brother, and did not want to be bothered with me. To me, the picture was a treasure. The counselor took one quick glance at the picture and exclaimed, "Look at you; you look like a tiny waif!" I did not expect this reaction. As the year progressed, she began to ask about my dad. I had no feelings to express about him, not yet anyway. They were still buried in there too deep to find. I got to a certain point, where I could hear the phone ring or open my mail without fear and dread, could buy some food and prepare and eat it without feeling so guilty I became nauseous, and then I stopped seeing her. My life became doable, for a time, until the car accident.

The process of healing has not been easy or quick. No fast drive-through trauma healing centers exist, that I know of anyway. I have wanted to give up at times, too painful, shameful, and condemned to let those feelings surface and be exposed. But I knew the options, continue limping along in life in sadness with no fulfillment, continue in illusion and dying in that state, or get the resolve to free myself from the tormenting thoughts, emotions, and physical reactions within.

It is time for healing. The exposure and uncovering of abuse in all facets of our society is a demonstration to the fact that the Spirit is exposing things that were hidden and not talked about, exposed to be examined and brought to light to create healing in the victims. It is time for each person to love himself or herself on the inside, not for what we show others on the outside. Our lives are gifts. Each gift an individual journey. Mine starts with me and will end with me. Yours starts with you and will end with you. And we will all touch many along the way.

FREE TO LOVE

Initially I started to write this book as a fiction romance novel. Sixty percent of books sold are romance novels. I thought this might be a way to tap into a new avenue of income. It did not take long for me to realize I did not have the imagination to write one. As the words came out, it became a story of my own life. This was surprising to me, but I knew I wanted it to be on healing and being free to love, especially one's self. Since I started writing before the trauma from the accident set in, and as healing has come, the story became a little bigger than it started out. My life took on a broader scope as I fitted the pieces together.

This book is not about trauma, but about the things that have affected our lives that keep us from being free to love and express our true selves. A large part of this expression is the desire and sometimes unhealthy "need" to have a relationship that we are looking to "complete" us. So much of our lives is tied up in this drive that we don't fill our being with finding our inner truth and self, but try to fill it with another. For women, maybe men too, this kind of living empty or unfulfilled is because we think we need someone to fill it, someone to be our all-in-all. Whether we are married or not, we feel this void as the lack of an exciting romantic relationship, something we all dream of and desire. There is a difference between a natural healthy desire for a relationship versus the need to fill our own void. Our culture molds our thoughts and behaviors into this pattern from infancy. It's easy to look at all media and realize the bombardment of the perfect romantic relationship, beginning with the cartoon characters and their magic princes and princesses.

My story is about finding and expressing the inner being. Who was I, or you, born to be? Do you ever find yourself feeling like your life is not what you want? Or life is just going by as you go through the motions? Or there is no joy in your heart, inside where it makes you feel good to be alive and wake up in the morning? Do you begin to look in the mirror and think the changes you see are not the person you are inside? Do you ever wake up in the middle of the night, look around, and wonder how your life got the way it is? Did you ever think your life would turn out like it has? How could you know what decisions would bring in the manifestation of your life as it is now? I have experienced all of these thoughts and feelings, many times.

Perhaps another word to describe this is identity. What does that mean to you? Who your parents are, or spouse is, or where you live? Most people, especially men, call their work their identity. If you asked someone to tell you who they are, they would first identify their occupation. Our persona has many outward expressions, but that is not our identity. When I say identity, I mean that person inside, the one you have to face when you are alone, or find some form of distraction so you can avoid the confrontation. I know for me, I kept myself very busy, with jobs, friends, church, and anything I could find as a way to not have to come face-to-face with me.

If you feel lost or anxious when by yourself, constantly in need of a "relationship," or long for something that you don't understand and cannot describe, then you and I are very much alike. If I can be set free to love, to love not only who I am all alone by myself, but to love others without it being the basis of my own value and self-worth or expecting anything back to boost me up, then I know it is possible for others to do also. I am sharing my story for anyone who is waiting and wanting for that someone to come into their lives, so that their life could begin. Not only begin, but have a meaning, a purpose, or to feel or find a value about oneself. Have you ever had this thought? *But I just want to know that there is someone out there that can love me.*

There are normal daily things that keep us distracted from our true inner thoughts. Things like the TV shows we watch, popular songs and stars, the latest fashion, sport heroes, and just the sort of busy things we keep our minds and days occupied with. In the end, all of those things are futile, meaningless distractions. Why do we allow our culture to cover depths of truth and fill our lives with shallow group identity and purpose? Anonymous groups are everywhere in our culture and draw people who are addicts of one form or another, ranging from alcoholism, codependency, eating disorders, gambling, drugs, such as Al-anon, Alcoholics Anonymous, Overeaters Anonymous. The list could go on. Plus, we are inundated from birth on, of the strong desire and need for material possessions and apparent financial success that will prove we are worthwhile. Our culture focuses on and tries to fix on the outside what is actually missing on the inside. Living the way we do, sometimes—maybe many times, something seems missing, a void we are trying to mask or soothe. No matter what we try to fill ourselves with, can we say inside we are truly at peace, fulfilled?

We all know that when it is dark, or late in the night, when we are alone, and we wonder why are we here, do we have a purpose—all the distractions in the world don't bring us the answers or the peace our inner self cries out for. Does all or any of this existence really have a purpose? If so, what is mine? Am I of any significance in the whole of this gigantic complex on the planet—just me, one little person?

I do remember as a child walking around outside looking up at the trees, agonizingly asking out loud, to my image of God, does any of this have a purpose? Perhaps that is because my mother locked me out of the house for the day, or swore at me again that she wished to god I had never been born. Did I have a purpose? Should I even be alive? How could my soul encompass what I had to wake up and face every day, plus find a purpose to want to wake up? What was enough to add meaning to my life?

We all want to believe that we have a purpose to fulfill while we are here on this earth. How do we find it? It is the journey of life and we all have our own to travel. I hope mine will be an encouragement for you to continue on yours, and to bring hope to those on their path or those who have not yet started on their journey. In this life, in spite of all the hardships we may experience, life is meant to have—and can have—deep personal value, meaning, and fulfillment.

Sharing My Story

"Write your story!" These were the words that came to me one day as I finished reading Betty J. Eadie's national bestseller, *Embraced By The Light*. I was on vacation in the Northwest in April of 1997 visiting my oldest son, his wife, and my newborn grandson. I had turned fifty in February, a definite milestone in a person's life. My first grandchild was born the end of March. And my dad died the day after the baby was born. The baby was one month old and I was on vacation to meet him. But I needed the time for refreshing and inner renewal after many long stressful hours at work over a two-year period and an unfulfilling personal life.

My daughter-in-law let me have time to myself. I probably did not appear as though I was a very excited "first-time" grandmother. Since they lived in a small house, her dad parked his camper trailer in the driveway for me to stay in so I could have some privacy. My son would go off to work early. I would hear his car drive away. Then I would get up and begin to read. I had taken eight books with me, quite a heavy load to lug across the country on an airplane. I had started these books, and had been just too exhausted over the previous two years to put my energy into completing them. When I first got to my son's, I spent the first three days sleeping, reading, thinking, eating, and walking in the evenings with their Golden Lab, Jessie. I would not even leave the camper until at least noon. After the third day of walking into the house at that time of the day, and looking at my daughter-in-law's face, I finally explained to her how grateful I was to have the time to myself, to get "rested."

This time period, a short two weeks, changed my life. It also started me on a course that was rockier and more revealing than anything that I could ever have imagined. I was reading books on inner healing, on how to rebuild your life, on spiritual experiences. I had started on a journey of inner healing when I began visiting the first counselor. Then I began studying and reading, and had continued on, each step being farther up the stairwell to what I hoped the ultimate top would be—no more deep inner loneliness, sadness, contempt, or inside crying. The books I had taken with me were all very interesting. As I finished the third one, Betty Eadie's book, I knew in my heart what I had to do. "Write your story!" The words were ingrained in my heart.

A year and a half later in July of 1998, I realized I let all that time go by and was only *thinking* about telling my story. Many, many thoughts entered my mind during this time. The first and foremost were shame and condemnation. Letting others in on the parts of my life that I never talked about made me realize how much of my life I was ashamed of, condemned about, and wanted to continue to hide. Not that I was a "bad" person. The shame came from the idea of exposing how I felt about myself and how I was treated, first by my family and then by my husband. I felt I let it happen, even though as a child I did not have the power to stand up for myself. It is difficult to begin to open up, to share your inner sanctum, and expose the shame you have kept buried about yourself for over fifty years. The result was that I did not want to "write my story" which also meant exposing my parental family. I was conditioned from a lifetime of their disapproval, learning we must appear good, and not hurt anyone else's feelings or make anyone mad. Just thinking of even telling anyone, even a counselor, the truth about my life, my insides would churn in agony.

There was one saving grace, however, that lived in the back of my mind, which I kept hearing. That grace finally propelled me to start. I went out for breakfast in the spring of 1998 with a friend of mine from church. Our sons had gone through school together. Jane and I always had found much in common, our beliefs, our interests, and our thoughts. As we were eating of course we were talking, often both at the same time. I began to tell her about a situation from my childhood, about living in the nursing home. I had gotten two lines into the conversation when she threw up her arms and said, "You have to write this down! You have to write this down! People need to hear this—you have to write it for others." Immediately I remembered the feeling of being in the camper at my son's. The same overwhelming sense of "writing my story" flooded back into my being. I had not done anything with it. And here it was again, only in spoken words, not the quiet voice that I had been entreated by the first time.

It has been difficult to know where to start or how to put it all together. Overcoming the shame of exposing my deep inner feelings and experiences, which can be categorized as abuse, has been harder than I could have imagined. And actually, I don't like the word abuse. It has almost become a buzzword in our society today. Many people use it. Many stories are around about the victims of that abuse. I'm sure it means different things to different people, because there are many types and forms of abuse.

All of the sciences are learning more about the connections between the spirit, mind, emotions, and our bodies. In studying these, it is evident that buried feelings and experiences are a major cause of adverse human behaviors and illnesses. I began to research about others who were on the road to healing, finding tidbits of truth here and there that continued to help me make steps. Our minds and bodies are set naturally to protect us from harm, whether that is physical, emotional, or mental. In this process, when we are unable to protect ourselves or understand what we may be experiencing, we make decisions, not based on the facts or the truth, but based on our perceptions at the time. This is especially true for children and even at a preverbal age. Something happens inside and we bury the truth, unable to cope, understand, or accept.

As children or teenagers, we have no adult sense of reasoning power to let us know what we experienced was right, wrong, abusive, or what. We just have an innate sense that something is not right, but are mostly unable to vocalize the feelings, especially to the one or ones who are our caretakers and we see as the source of our lives. So to compensate, our bodies and our subconscious mind create splits, part of us splits off from our awareness, it is a form of survival. How many times have you heard of bad or horrible experiences happening to people, but they can't remember them? These splits often become traps for our emotions or memories held in our subconscious or bodies. Usually we are not even aware this is happening. After it goes on for so long, if we are able to evaluate our thoughts, actions, and reactions, patterns of behavior can be recognized. These can be manifested as physical illness, emotional or mental illness, addictions, relationship issues, almost any human expression that shows something is creating an internal warning. It is when that inside pain, the empty feeling, or knowing something is missing begins to echo loudly in our lives that we try to force our lives into change, healing. If we listen, we will find our innate is crying to be who we were created to be—that whole person living a fulfilling and meaningful life. Healing is possible and a reality, no matter what your story may have been.

PART TWO

THE REAWAKENING OF MY HEART

At the age of fifty, I had given up the idea of ever finding real inner happiness and fulfillment, not only in and for myself, but most especially from another person—a man—who would want me and who could love me, for no other reason than just because I am me. The term of soul mate or love of my life would express this well. I thought I was too old, had watched my life, my chances for love be destroyed by various situations. With the thought of giving up on this hope, dream, and desire—which is innate within each of us—life seemed routine and humdrum, lacking the deep companionship that makes things fun. And just when I had given up, and thought that all there was going to be left in my life was to watch my body grow saggy and wrinkly, be alone, and just go to work every day until I retire, and after that I did not want to imagine what, someone walked by my desk at work one day, someone that I noticed. And my heart leaped inside.

The introduction of Adam into my life became the avenue of bittersweet feelings and reactions within me, ranging from enchantment and euphoria, to estrangement and despair. Little did I know that lurking beneath the surface of my nice friendly demeanor, a multitude of emotions were waiting for the perfect opportunity to make themselves known. It started ever so slowly at first, always after an interlude of some sort with Adam. Either after seeing him in the plant, talking with him, or being with him, I was so overwhelmed by feelings of insecurity and fear of rejection that I would be beside myself, unable to think, unable to make it even through the next hours without some sort of assuredness or consolation. I always called on Barb. She was always there to talk me through and help me back to a point of centering. Barb was the benefits coordinator where I worked. We had been friends for years and went to the same church. She had even taught my sons in junior high. I could say anything to her. She had been the person who guided me to the first counselor I visited and helped me through that difficult time. Barb and I were good friends, loving to laugh and enjoy life together. Barb became my anchor when the emptiness and doubts were erupting and overwhelming. During the time of Adam in my life, as these empty lost feelings would surface, they would often attach themselves to specific childhood memories, like I was reliving something from my past, even though it was relating to Adam that made it surface. I can't even begin to say how often they surfaced, probably numerous times daily. If he failed to notice me, if he did not answer his phone, if I did not understand something he said, would he want to go out with me again. Anything and everything surfaced a deep need and void that made me feel so empty and lost. Letting myself have feelings for Adam was one of the most vulnerable places that I had ever put myself into. I knew at the time I had to find some answers, to fill the emptiness that made me feel incomplete, needy, with no identity on my own.

Between Adam and the car accident, I realized I was not only not a whole person, I had so many pieces and fragments I did not know what was me and what was not me. I was never allowed the freedom to find, to express, or to be who I was. I had no identity. This became the unfolding of my story, filling in the voids, connecting the dots, learning to find my voice, identify my heart, my feelings. Searching, seeking, exposing, crying—these became my life for a time period. And one day, a memory that kept repeating in the back of my mind like a broken record came back, triggered by an insecure situation I was in. But this time my reaction was different. I felt something different inside where this memory could not trigger its normal excruciating angst. I knew healing all the fragments of my life was on the way.

Five a.m.! The alarm doesn't even have to go off, and I would wake up. I would wake up and wait for the alarm to go off. Then I would shut it off. I would try to go back to sleep, trying to find a rest for my mind for a short period of time, before the day and all the responsibilities that were waiting at the office started crowding in on me, making me feel like I never could be caught up, causing me to lose an awareness of life. Every day was the same way. For six months, every morning began the same. Every night, the same restless turnings, waking at least every other hour, often times more, to look at the clock, hoping that somehow time would ride off into the dark horizon and I could find peace and rest. Even my cats didn't know what to do with me at times. *Before*, they had always been waiting patiently for my alarm to go off at 5:30, sitting and waiting for me to get out of bed to serve their breakfast. *This was before Adam came to our workplace.*

Working for one of the largest corporations in the country had benefits, and also had non-benefits, like every job I suppose. Our company, as a maker of interior automobile parts, was always on the up-and-down of attitudes, morale, and expectations swinging with the cycle of car sales, which were influenced by a lot of different factors. It was an atmosphere that caused the employees to see every day as another day to get through, to wait for the time to go home or get the paycheck. It was a cycle that never ended, and I had been in it for ten years.

Even with the downfalls, the attitudes, the long hours,

and the heavy workload, I tried to find a challenge, tried to make the best of the responsibilities as opportunities to learn new things, improve the ways of the plant. I had been quite successful in my roles at the plant. The company had been in the process of massive internal restructuring for at least three years, cutting heads, rearranging departments, trying new forms of management. I had been moved to four totally different positions during the ten years of my employment there, and was moved at a moment's notice. That was the world of the corporate automotive supplier. With new management within the last year, new requirements were not only coming, they were being demanded. Work to me was a means to an end, and I lost track of what that end was as my beliefs in the American dreams and fairy tale stories of life became twisted into the reality of my life. Long hours of work filled up my time and helped to keep my mind from other things, like the pace and path my life was going. Work was the perfect escape and excuse.

I was always, it seemed, working toward getting my life together. After a bad marriage of sixteen years, I had been single for thirteen years. I liked being able to provide for myself. I liked being able to take responsibility for my own life. And I liked being alone. In fact, even though there was this hidden desire in the depth of my heart for "someone," my outward appearance was one of self-sufficiency, no vulnerability, no need, no desire—just let me be and let me live my life.

For an international corporation with eight hundred employees, it was not uncommon for visitors—consultants, corporate personnel, and corporate clients—to frequently visit the facility. In fact, it was so common, you never thought about the new faces you saw. You knew they were there doing their job today, and tomorrow they would be gone. So you just tended to your business, and did what needed to be done. In November 1997, something happened that brought a new focus and interest, an interest that began to counteract the routine demands of my work life. The corporation hired a special outside consultant group to work in our plant to assist in raising the Return-On-Sales (ROS) to twenty percent. This group consisted of eight men. The faces would change at times, depending on what had to be done. They were so busy, there to work, not socialize in any way.

My world was busy, working long hours at the computer, ten hours if I was lucky, sometimes more at my own choice, sometimes weekends. The department I worked in was located in the most trafficked area of the plant, very close to the front offices where most salaried employees and all visitors entered the building. I sat at the conjunction of the front lab and upstairs old engineering area. It was like having a desk in the middle of Grand Central Station or a very active beehive. The ability to concentrate on my job took most of my energy and focus. Not only the traffic, but the noise from the plant, all the machinery and equipment, made a continual blast as large injection molds and monstrous roto ovens began the production of parts that moved on down the assembly lines.

Our plant was gearing up for QS9000 certification, an incredibly important acquisition for a manufacturing facility that produced parts for the Big Three automotive makers, since it was the international quality standard for all production documentation. The companies could not purchase our parts unless we met these specifications. In our plant, this meant rewriting hundreds of job descriptions and data specifications to the required format, identifying and tracking each revision in a database, and having them "look" professional to display on the production line for the employees.

I was totally focused on work, too busy and too tired to pay much attention to anything out of the needed duties I had to fulfill. My personal life was on hold too, held at bay by all of the personal disappointments I encountered along the way. I found refuge in letting my life be drained by the demands of my job so I could not even try to think about doing much after hours. But, there was the day in November, with the busy traffic through all of the doors, there was a moment when I looked up and was astonished to see someone whom I had never seen before. My heart leaped inside, and I thought, *where did he come from?* I waited for him to come back and go upstairs to where the consultants had finally landed after being moved several times. He came back by my desk but did not notice me. I went back into my world.

A few weeks after this, right before Christmas, I had occasion to meet this person. His name was Adam. He was assigned to work on a project I had originally assisted in implementing and maintaining in the plant, downtime collection and analysis to be used as an evaluation tool by the production managers. Adam was introduced to me to find out about the forms, downtime codes, and reports that we used. He was kind, but seemed focused on work. He shook my hand as we were introduced. Something inside of me did not want to let his hand go.

After this initial meeting, I went on vacation to the Northwest to visit my oldest son and his family. It was my grandson's first Christmas. I thought about Adam once in a questioning romantic way, then pushed him out of my mind. I thought how illogical and impractical to even think he would notice me. I had let the effects of my personal life and the stress from work take its toll on me. For most of my life I had exercised as a means to maintain my health, loving to run, bike, do yoga, or try some new form of fitness. Over the last two years I had became lethargic, not exercising, not caring how I looked, and had given to eating fast easy food. This change in my behavior and attitude caused me to be thirty pounds and three sizes above what I considered my normal appearance to be. This appearance was important to me not to attract the attention of men, but because it made me feel good about myself, a self I had quit caring about.

In mid January, the "team" was started. There was Adam—the champion. Management handpicked the team to assist Adam in setting up a new plant-wide downtime system. And of course, I was on the team. I remember watching him in the first meeting. I was absolutely spellbound by the sight and sound of him. He had a great presentation, even though I did not hear a word that he said. Every so often, as I was looking at the handout or someone asked me a question, when I would look back at Adam, I had the sense that from across the room he was trying to look at the ring I wore on my left hand. Every weekend, he would go home to Texas, and come back on Mondays.

The first weekend after the meeting with Adam, I woke up in the middle of Saturday night, thinking about him, having feelings and desires for him, wondering why I should be thinking of him like this. I had been attracted to other men, and had had a boyfriend for several years. There was nothing that had transpired with Adam that would cause me to begin to wander off in my mind with him about anything other than work. Besides, there was a man in my church that I had been interested in for several years. Sometimes I would wonder why, but I persisted in maintaining this thought, even though nothing ever materialized. I am one of those people that let go of others with great difficulty, even when there is no reason to hold on. As long as I had someone in my mind, it was much easier to push others away, and to push feelings away. It was much easier to live in a futuristic, fantasy hope than to face reality, at this point in my life. And somehow over the years, my lack of success in relationships, my perspective of lack of success in my whole life, made me vulnerable to wanting to please others to a point where I did not trust myself or any of my feelings. I wanted to be free of having to make any such decision on my own. So I maintained this interest for several reasons I guess, my religion became a safe place for me and I did not have to expose myself to anyone—I did not have to worry about rejection and disapproval.

I will never forget the first time I talked to Adam on a personal level, rather than work matters, right at the beginning of the team starting. It was early spring, chilly and damp, and I was leaving the plant for the day. On purpose, I went out the front of the plant so I could walk by the outside eating and smoking area where Adam and his associates congregated after shifts changed. As I walked by, he was out there with his co-workers just as I hoped he might be. I glanced over at him. He motioned for me to come over to him. He left his group and we stood together, privately, openly. He started talking about work, then quickly changed the topic and began to tell me about his personal life. He lived in a suburb of Houston in a 4,400 square-foot home, alone, bordering a golf course, and surrounded by trees. Everyone in his neighborhood had traded their Mercedes for Lexus when Lexus came out. He went on and on, telling me about his lifestyle, things he had done. He had been everywhere, it seemed to me, played soccer and traveled everywhere, even to England to play soccer. I thought about his house and my little four hundred square foot apartment. I had seen people like him in the movies and read about them in books. The more he talked, the more I shrank inside of myself. I was shivering the whole time we talked. I wanted to go home. Our conversation finally ended. As I walked away, I said inside of myself, "Lord, I never want to talk to that man again." Just as quickly, that still small voice answered, "Your world is too small, Linda." Thank goodness I did talk to him again—and—on a personal level.

My mind was beginning to be full of Adam continually. Occasionally I would see him in the plant, talking to the maintenance men as he worked on scheduling and training them to think about their roles in a more positive, important way. He was always business, never giving any notice that I was around. However, I could not help but notice him. When I walked through the plant, I began to hope that I would see him. Just seeing him was an unbelievable charge and thrill to my being, even though he never seemed to notice me.

There was a time period of about three weeks between the first and second meeting. The plant rearranged the office personnel again. My desk was moved to an upstairs department, the new engineering department, the old one where Adam was stationed being in the front of the building, the new one on the side, but they were not joined. My new location was much quieter and much more private, not visible to the eight hundred people who tromped through the plant every day. Then late one Friday, Adam was walking through our area, an area that was now out of his normal route, and stopped by my desk. I was stunned. He sat down, said he was leaving for the weekend, but would be back on Monday to get things going with the team. I felt awkward, and as I watched him walk away, something inside of me longed for him to stay.

A week later I was late going to the second team meeting. Needless to say, I wanted off the team. I sat at my desk, waiting for another employee to get out of my boss's office so I could ask my boss for permission to get off the team, mulling over what I would say. I knew I had no good excuse, and he would want one. I tried to convince myself I did not want to participate due to the attitudes of several of the employees on the team, and my work load, actually knowing what it would entail to revamp our downtime system. But the real reason I did not want to admit to anyone, especially to myself, was because of the strong attraction I felt toward Adam. I was so attracted to him, I was afraid my feelings would carry me to a place which I kept in strict control—a place in my heart which felt like a dark room, locked up, with no light and no air, but a place where my heart would not end up hurt or disappointed. Luckily, maybe it was fate or that word "destiny," I had to stay on, and it became the avenue for our communication and contact for the months to come.

After fifteen minutes of waiting outside my boss's office, I knew I had to take responsibility to do what was asked of me. With great reluctance, I took my notepad and went to the meeting. It was in the area where Adam was located, and inside a small partitioned room. I dragged my feet all the way. When I opened the door, my heart started to beat hard and fast. I sat down, and could barely stand to look at Adam. He was at the opposite end of a six-foot by three-foot table. Six other people, all women, were seated, three along each side of the table. The only place for me to sit was directly opposite him, on the end. I kept trying to look at the other people, afraid what I was feeling inside would show on my face. I was so relieved when the maintenance coordinator, Bob, came in later than I did and sat beside me. I tried distracting myself by talking and joking with him on the side. This was totally rude on my part, to say the least, not only not listening to Adam, but talking to Bob when Adam was trying to talk to others. There was one point in the meeting when I had to say something. Two of the women said almost simultaneously, "You have a very soft voice, and Adam has a very soft voice. It is hard to hear you." They first pointed to Adam, then to me. I just sat there and looked at him, trying to be nonchalant. At the end of the meeting Adam gave out work assignments. He assigned the other six women to work on codes, three people to each assignment. All six turned and looked at me, and said, "Well, Linda does not have anything to do." I looked at Adam and said, "Bob doesn't either. I guess that means we just can come here and watch." At that point Adam tossed a form, which he had created on the computer, halfway across the table and asked if I could work on the form. He said that he would work with me on it. I was speechless. I thought, *Oh, my god.*

For the next two weeks, I saw the back of him walking through the plant. He was very busy. At one point I saw him coming down the stairs from a meeting, the stairs I had to go up. I was hoping he would see me so I could ask him about the form. At the last moment as he was turning to go into the break room, his head turned. I caught his eye, motioning for him. He stopped. I went up to him, asking about the form. As I stood there close to hear him due to all of the noise in the plant and the protective earplugs, I felt like I had just taken off into a space where there was nothing that existed except him. I looked closely at his features: his intense blue eyes; his trimmed reddish-blonde hair; his expressionless, straight face—that could be interpreted as stern; his mouth, not defying any emotions; his neck, which was right at my eye-level. I noticed his extremely straight-backed and disciplined stance. I noticed his hands, very clean and manicured. He gestured as he spoke. There was a very nice ring on the fourth finger of each hand. When he walked away, I was oblivious to everyone and everything around me.

As I found my way to my desk, consuming thoughts about him overwhelmed my mind. My heart pounded.

I began to learn Adam's routine in the plant. He was very dependable and very consistent. He always held an impromptu meeting with the maintenance crew around three p.m. in the middle of the plant, going over issues with them as the shifts passed responsibilities from one group to the next. I started planning my times that I had to go out into the plant to see if I could get lucky and catch him in one of these meetings. I would try to not look too out-of-the-ordinary as I glanced at him as I walked by. I changed the route I usually took and I began to watch the clock regularly, to make my "rounds."

Every time I saw him, even though he did not notice me or talk to me, I felt like I was in a timeless, weightless space of float-ing. I was in awe of how I was beginning to feel inside. It was one of the most exhilarating feelings I had ever had. But I had to keep it all hidden because I did not allow myself to have feelings. Feelings were something that I had shut down. When feelings started for Adam, especially ones that embodied anything sensual or sexual, I began an inner struggle and turmoil that became the prompting for the unfolding of my story.

This new excitement about Adam in my life had another impact on me. It made me begin to see what I had let happen to myself over the last few years, on a physical level, of not caring for myself. I bought some new clothes, changing in my baggy T-shirts and jeans for more colorful sweaters and slacks. I did a few other things. I began to look at myself in the mirror in the mornings. I got a perm and began to put on a little makeup. I began to feel like I wanted to look pretty. I began exercising again. My favorite thing to do was to go outside around eight or nine o'clock at night and run-walk. Slowly, my body began to change. However, part of me was so euphoric inside about Adam these other changes were very minimized to me at the time. With all of these changes going on, on the outside of me, inside the changes unveiled more and more vulnerability. I was beginning to feel like I was putting myself in a place where I was vulnerable to not be responded to, bypassed or rejected for another, or simply just not worthy of any attention at all. The inner insecurities were magnifying. I did not let them show on the outside. But on the inside tormenting thoughts and fears crept in, feelings and emotions that made the emptiness—the void—inside of me feel like the Grand Canyon, a deep chasm that left me feeling stranded, stuck, hopeless, and helpless.

I had debated for days, agonizing over if I should say something to Adam about spending time with him after working hours. He had mentioned a girlfriend once when we were talking about a recent storm where he lived, but had not mentioned her again. He increasingly became more attentive to me. Meeting times between us increased. To me, the attraction felt so strong, I felt like it was booming out of me like a radio broadcast. I was constantly trying to resolve, or I should say squelch these feelings for Adam. It became a tug of war, and I had no peace. The only thing that kept coming to my mind was, "If you try, what do you have to lose? You need to take the initiative and see what will happen." I did not want to decide if I should "relate" to Adam other than work. This decision was too big. I held a lot of hurt and blame for a bad marriage and what that did to my children. I lived in great fear of making a mistake again. The consequences were too great. "Sometimes the person you marry is not necessarily the person you wake up with," my mother-in-law started saying to me two days after the marriage. Within the week, I knew what she was talking about. I wanted God to make the decision about Adam for me. I was afraid to be responsible for my own feelings and actions, wanting to escape blame, condemnation, and the consequences if the decision turned out to be another nightmare and not the fairy tale.

As it turned out, my church overseer along with his wife provided the answer for me. I had known Scott and Julie for ten years. I had talked to them about Adam. I had also previously talked to them about the man from church. They were a strong spiritual support during my divorce. We were church "family." I had taken an afternoon off work early in the week and had just stepped out of the health food store. As I was driving away, I heard someone yelling my name, running down the middle of the street after my car. I lived in a very small community, so it was easy to see people you knew. I stopped in the middle of the street and rolled the window down. The sun was warm. Scott had his whole arm bandaged and in a sling, from nearly cutting his arm off in a carpentry accident. As soon as we finished talking about his mishap, the words came out of his mouth, "Linda, I know that you want to be pursued in a relationship, but you don't know how long this guy is going to be around. So you need to take the initiative and see what will happen."

I drove away stunned. It was like he read my mind. My stomach went into knots and stayed that way, just full of nervous energy and twitching. Fears and unsettling thoughts began to race through my mind of what I would say. Would Adam look at me like I was crazy? Whatever anyone can imagine in circumstances like these, I probably did imagine. I thought about Scott's words for several days. I decided to take some action. I decided that I would approach Adam on a personal level. On Friday, the day I decided was "A" day, I did not see Adam at work. I thought he must have had to go back to Texas a day early.

That weekend was long and agonizing. It was Mother's Day weekend. Mother's Day, as any holiday, was always difficult for me after my family broke up. I thought of Adam often. My stomach was queasy and still full of knots as I thought of approaching him on Monday. But on Monday as I went about my normal routine in the plant, there was no Adam. I saw all of his co-workers. I walked through the old engineering area several times where the consultants had their computers and equipment. Even the car he usually drove was not where he normally parked. My heart sank inside. I was frantic. I ran into Barb's office to talk to her. She knew my feelings for Adam. I would call her or go to her office for help or advice when the intense anxiety or empty feelings I experienced after seeing Adam or not being noticed by him would rise up within me. This time I thought perhaps Adam was never coming back. Of course then I would have my "answer from God" for sure. Barb was, as always, very objective, very calmly saying, "Maybe it's something you don't know about."

By mid afternoon I could not stand the unknown any longer and stopped to talk to his team leader and ask about him. I pretended I had something from our work to show him. As it turned out, Adam had ended up in the hospital on Thursday night, the night before "A" day. I thought, *oh, how awful, to be in a strange city, and spend four days in the hospital where no one knows you.* I decided to call Adam in the hospital. I don't know where that spurt of guts and bravery came from. He, of course, seemed shocked to hear from me. Why wouldn't he be? He said his gut went into these wrenching spasms that did not stop. His co-workers did not know what to do, so they took him to the hospital. Of course, tests were run. They could find nothing and suggested it was some popcorn he had eaten. He said he had never had anything like that before. After learning more about Adam's life, I realized how painful this must have been for him. He had been in the Army for ten years, was on the boxing team, and had to run ten miles a day. He knew what pain was.

On the phone I talked about being in the hospital over a holiday weekend. He said, "Well, actually I kind of enjoyed it. After the pain stopped and they stopped doing tests, that is. I pulled out a novel that I had started on over a year ago, and began working on it again." My heart leaped. A novel! Someone who also loves to write! I told him about my children's books I was writing. We now had the perfect conversation topic and interest between us. He had his computer and email at the hospital, so at my initiative we exchanged email addresses, and I began this form of communication with him.

To explain my love of writing: I am writing children's books. My children's books came alive in the summer of 1997. This experience was completely independent from the "writing my story" experience. When I finally realized this man in my church was not going to discover me, I was crushed beyond hope. I was lost in living in the fantasy of giving my sons the perfect family life that we never had, even though by this time they were adults and well on their way into building their own futures. With this loss of hope, the feeling about my life and the purpose of my life grew dismal. I always attached my purpose to other people. I basically felt my life was over. I felt old and done. I was tired of just having jobs to keep my life going, I had lost my career drive which had never been that strong anyway. One hot summer evening I walked across my backyard to the convenience mart on the corner. On the way back I walked under the large pin oaks in the back yard where two squirrel families lived. I loved to watch the squirrels play in these trees. An idea leaped into my mind of a story about a small animal and her animal friends. My mind felt

*like electricity was racing through it with the excitement of these
characters. I went into my apartment, sat down, and thought
about this. I had learned at a young age to not be spontaneous,
to be cautious, think everything through, and wait to see what
happens, and hide until something did. I sat there holding back
this excitement, resisting writing anything down. I said, "Okay,
if there is something to this, I'll still have it tomorrow." After
work the next day I sat at my computer. Within half an hour this
wonderful story came out. I was amazed. This was the birth of
my children's books.*

Adam came back to work the next week. I had decided
I would talk with him after our next team meeting. To my
surprise, he stopped by my desk a few minutes early on the
way to our meeting. He asked what I thought of the team
progress. Obviously I had broken the ice by calling him
and initiating our new email connection. Now was a great
opportunity to change the subject to more personal topics.
We quickly exchanged a little information about our writing
as we walked to the meeting. I showed him a picture of my
grandson. I don't even know how my grandson got into the
conversation. I think it was subconscious on my part because
I wanted Adam to know that I came with obligations and
responsibilities in my life, and that I was also older than I
looked.

After the meeting he stopped by my table and we chat-
ted casually. We were talking about doing something for the
meetings in a few weeks. I said, "Well, I might not be here."
His face looked full of concern and questions. "Why? Where
will you be?" As I looked around the room two employees
were so carefully trying to find excuses to stay in the room,
doing this and doing that, so I tried to be careful and very
nonchalant. However, just looking at Adam made that
impossible for me. I said I was going on vacation to see my

older son and his family. He looked relieved. He positioned himself in a way against one of the filing cabinets behind him that told me he was in no hurry to leave the room. So I turned my back on the other employees and tried to talk very softly. I said, "Well, would you consider doing something after work hours some time? Like maybe go out for coffee or something? That is if you don't already have a girlfriend." Adam's immediate response was "Yes!" Then he said, "But it might be difficult. I don't know for sure when I'll be back." He said his employers were having meetings and making decisions and he may have to stay in Houston for a time.

I was totally devastated. The excitement of seeing and the expectation of possibly being with this man made my whole life begin to change. I was beginning to feel something new inside, like a seed in the spring after the hard winter, the seed will spring up with new life, and every ray of sunshine and drop of water adds to the beauty of its growth. Adam walked me back to my desk. Then he was gone for the weekend, and maybe much longer. I did not know.

I don't remember what that weekend was like for me. I do remember on Monday morning how drab work seemed knowing Adam would not be there. I went on my usual morning routine about nine a.m. throughout the plant, checking things, picking up reports, and delivering mail. I looked over at one of the large injection machines as I approached it. There was Adam on the walkway of the machine talking with a maintenance person. He looked at me with a huge smile and inviting eyes. I just looked at him, shocked. I could not even smile, I was so stunned. His smile quickly faded and he quickly looked back down at his paper. I felt like my heart had been ripped out. I thought he had lied to me, after I had begun to be open to him. Needless to say, my morning became very long. I could not concentrate on work.

Several hours later, on another trip through the plant, I ran into Adam very unexpectedly. He stopped me and planted himself in front of me. He started to talk. I could not believe how friendly he was. This was not his normal formal and careful demeanor and behavior. He was very smiley and chatty. It was obvious he did not want to run off quickly. This was a difficult and improper place to hold a conversation, especially a personal one. The plant manager came up to me needing a certain report. Adam stepped in between us and said, "Well, when we finish here." I was speechless. The plant manager just looked at him and walked away.

Adam apologized, saying that he knew he would be back this week, but no one else was supposed to know. There was something going on between him, his employer, and our company regarding negotiations. He was now the only consultant from his firm that would be working at our facility. He said, "Well, you know what you said about doing something after work? If you still want to do that, I will be here this week, until Wednesday. Or we could wait until next week." I thought, *Hum—he's testing me.* I said, "Well, let's just do it this week then." We made plans to go out. Tuesday I was going to meet him at seven p.m. in the lobby of his hotel.

My anxiety in getting ready to meet Adam was overwhelming. I was shaking inside of myself, not only due to the excitement of seeing him, but because shutting out dating men had became a safe place for me to be. Barb came over to help me get ready. She helped me pick out my clothes, made sure my hair looked okay, and painted my nails. She was trying to help my nervousness.

Adam was staying in a downtown hotel. I parked in the parking ramp and met him in the lobby. He was ten minutes late. I became anxious thinking he would not show up. He had just gotten a haircut and was nervous that it was cut too short. I really could not tell the difference—he looked great to me whatever. The next thing he did was hand me a pile of papers—part of his novel. He asked me to read it and maybe we could work on it together. He wanted my feedback. I knew then this would be more than a one-time meeting. We got into his rental car and started driving around the city. I was showing him some areas he had not seen. First thing he did was to tell me he had a girlfriend. I really panicked. This was the one stipulation I had brought up. I did not believe in violating relationships. He immediately told me he would not marry her. It was easy to sense he was toying with ending the relationship. We ended up driving to a lake, my favorite spot, and then to eat and talk. Well—he talked—I listened. I had so little confidence in myself, I kept quiet, a very safe spot I learned from early in life. We had a great time, and kept everything on a friendship level. We decided to go out again. We always had his book to discuss, even though his discussions about work and his life could have been endless.

I could hardly sleep that night, just thinking about him. It was exhilarating driving to work the next day, the thought of seeing him, where and when. It was also excruciatingly painful—deep inside where parts of me felt like pieces of a splattered rowboat tossing in a vast, stormy ocean, lost without a centering magnet to pull and hold me together. It now became clear that Adam was becoming a part of my personal life, a part that I was beginning to want to be more than an acquaintance or friendship. With this also came the realization of the deep vulnerability and fear of rejection that could be part of this. As time went on, we continued to see each other more at work and after hours. Every time together became more enthralling than the first. We got into a routine of two favorite places. One of the easiest and most frequently visited places we found ourselves at was in the hotel where he stayed. Between the bar and restaurant there was a private room we liked. It was a place where we could be free from anyone seeing us, and we could just relax. His favorite spot was in a city twenty miles away, a fine dining restaurant in the top floor of the downtown event center. This was really nice. We would spend leisurely time just enjoying each other's company, always maintaining a friendship level. I knew he really liked me, it was easy to tell, but he never once crossed a boundary of expressing or showing anything more than being a friend. At one dinner, he even talked about me working with him in the future as his editor. He was actually in the process of writing two other novels. When he said this, I knew he was seeking a way to continue a relationship even if he was no longer part of the plant.

Our conversations always centered around work, his writings, or his life. I learned a lot about him. He lived quite a fascinating and multi-faceted life, as different from mine as night and day. The more he talked, the less I wanted to talk about myself. His life was enthralling, exciting, and big. Mine was very small, very safe. I loved hearing about his life, I never shared mine. How could a man who had dated gorgeous women who were corporate executives be interested in little town, simple me! He had quite a social lifestyle, one that he loved. But that did not mean I could not enjoy him for when he was here, giving me attention. I could never imagine myself in Adam's world, and knew he would never be content in mine. Yet, that could not stop the feelings, the longing, and the desire to have him look at me with those intense blue eyes. You could never tell what he was feeling or thinking, but those blue eyes on occasion made him appear vulnerable.

Then one week in the fall, very unexpectedly to him and to me, Adam came back from Texas on a Monday and said this was his last week. While he was home over the weekend, he found out that our company had ended the contract. He was not to come back. I was shocked. He wanted to meet several times that week, if it worked out. Our final night together Adam made a decision between spending it with me or going out to dinner with the international corporate vice president, a person who was highly impressed with Adam. He sneaked away from work early so we could be together. Maybe not a good company or career based decision, but one that let me know he was driven, as I was, to be together. We just never spoke of any feelings for each other. He would not violate where he was. He was not free to speak. I was unwilling. He wanted to come to my house that night. I lived in a small town twenty miles away. I would not let him. I did not want him to see my life.

We went to his favorite spot, the restaurant in the top of the downtown event center twenty miles away. I was full of anxiety, wanting to know there would be more. Realizing it did not matter at that point what he thought of me since this was apparently the end, I was actually more relaxed and talked more. He even commented about it on the way home that I talked more that night. I could tell he enjoyed that. When we said goodbye that last night, we shared a sweet and sincere embrace, while in my heart longing for so much more. He said that I should be in his "office" first thing in the morning. We did try to keep it somewhat discreet at work. This was his last day. I helped him get everything ready to go. He also shared a document with me that he had been working on. It was a two-year proposal for him to set up our plant as the base for long-term training for the company's facilities nationwide. He planned to bring in groups to our plant for training. In the proposal he had requested for me to be his assistant. He seemed to have a confidence that it would be accepted.

When he left he handed me his card, writing his home phone number on it, saying to call him. I looked at him, and said, "No, I probably will not."

He looked at me somewhat stunned—finally an expression on his face I could read. He said, "If the other 'issue' (which was the word he used when he referred to his girlfriend) answers, just say you are calling about work."

Again, I said, "No, I probably won't."

Then Adam answered, "Well, you'll have to call me about the book anyway, to work on the book, so here." I took the card.

Then he left. The emptiness, the void, the loneliness set in. I heard from him a few times during the next couple weeks, as he was trying to get his proposal accepted. Then his company sent him off to Michigan, and his life was on another path. We emailed a few times, very infrequently on his part. I threw his card and phone number away. He even sent me the final version of the chapters of his book that we had reviewed together. He wanted to know what I thought about it. I emailed back that it was good. Someone had done excellent editing work on it, and I wondered who that was.

We emailed a few more times. Then he vanished out of my life. I was left to face what I was afraid to open up to at the beginning, letting someone come in and then be gone. Even though I really did not let him into my life, I let him into my feelings. I just never let my feelings show. I can't explain the sadness I experienced over the next weeks and months. I had a deep longing for him and the attention he gave me, and I grieved.

THE CAR ACCIDENT

After Adam left, my life felt really empty, not only my life, but me, inside. I longed for the way he used to look at me. I longed for the anticipation of being able to see him at various times throughout the day. I longed for the evening phone calls. I longed for our times together, sitting across from each other at the dinner table, talking, and looking intensely at each other.

My daily life fell into a routine, going to work, stopping at the university track and field house for some exercise, going home, and spending the evenings in loneliness. Barb had been going through a divorce and had a new boyfriend who lived in another state. Many of my evenings became full of being with her. We did a lot of laughing and lots and lots of talking about her new boyfriend. Our friendship became even more important to me, kind of like a lifeline support. She and I did not talk about Adam any more.

Then in mid October of 1998, around six p.m., I was on my way home from walking on the track at the field house. It was dusk. The weather was a little misty. I was driving through an intersection that had a blind spot on an incline for oncoming traffic. Speeding up from that blind spot was a car going way too fast to be going through an intersection and making a turn. The car turned in front of me, hitting me head-on, no warning, no sign to me of it even coming, no lights on. At first I was stunned and did not know what had happened, just knew my car stopped. In fact it felt like it had jumped backwards. I looked up and saw the car in front of me. I thought, *Oh, no, this can't be happening, it can't be real.* I tried to reach up and turn off my ignition to stop my car. My hands would not work. Then I tried to roll down the window because I could feel a tight constraint on my chest. I was having trouble breathing. I could not make my hands work. Then the pain set in, in my middle back, in the back of my neck, and in the middle of my chest. The girl driving the other car was banging on my window asking me if I was all right. I tried to yell out to her that I could not breathe, to get help. She started running around in circles within the intersection, screaming, and holding her head.

I put my head back on the headrest and tried to focus on breathing. It was hard. Everything around me had become very dim. It seemed like I was looking through a gray-colored cloud. My hearing began to seem like I was listening through a long and distant tube coupled to my ear. I felt like my life was swimming in a fishbowl within my car, and I was entrapped in it. I thought of my spiritual overseer and the head of our church, felt their spirits in the fishbowl with me, and tried to keep my thoughts on them. My body felt numb. I thought I was dying. I said to the Lord, "Lord, I would not be afraid to die if I could find you, if I could feel your Presence." I had read of others who had near-death or actual-death experiences. I was waiting for some sign from the heavens, so I could let go of my breath.

Instead of a glorious light or angel, two things instantly became very, very clear and real to me—my sons. It came as a quick flash, but was more real than reality. I knew the Lord had met me. And in this flash I gained a new understanding of living that continues to unfold. We could do many things in this life; we could be many things to many people. But in the end we're held accountable for the relationships and purposes that are important to God, not necessarily what we might deem as important for us to have or do. Time began to seem eternal, never moving, during those few moments. I knew I wanted to—and was supposed to—live.

Then my car door opened. A woman took my arm and started to monitor my pulse. She was a medical doctor who had been sitting at the stoplight watching the accident. Since I was over fifty, heart failure during an accident was a major concern. She had a young daughter in her car who was using her cell phone to call 911. The doctor was asking questions about the pain. Then the rear door behind me opened. A young woman jumped into the back seat and held my neck. She was a paramedic also on her way home from work. It did not take long for the ambulance to arrive, but because of the possibility of neck or back injuries, they were hesitant to move me from the car. We had to wait for the rescue unit. I remember hearing the sirens from the large rescue unit approaching. I could vaguely see it as it parked kitty-corner within the intersection. The emergency team went to work to put a backboard behind me to get me out of the car. I was vaguely aware of all that was going on around me.

It was while listening to these voices around me, all trying to help me, that I finally heard what I had been waiting for. It was not that great flash of light so I could let go of this life and go on to the other side. I heard the still small voice echoing from without, but resounding from the depths of my being. It was very loud and very real, "I'm all around you, Linda, in all of these people who are trying to help you." I tried to look intently into the faces of everyone. My eyes could not focus. I could only vaguely hear them. The policeman came over and said I had nothing to worry about, that the other driver was fully responsible for the accident. It seemed like hours before I was put into the ambulance. In the background, I could still hear the hysterical screaming of the girl that caused the accident as they closed the ambulance doors.

The ambulance team decided to take me to university hospitals instead of where I had requested to go. I was thinking of insurance coverage. They were thinking of the possibility of very serious injuries. It was on the ambulance ride, after I was able to focus and be a little more aware, when I saw the concern in the faces of the emergency workers, I became afraid of what kind of injuries I might have. The sensations of numbness began to give way to the pain—the damaged muscles, tendons, and nerve endings were excruciatingly painful. That pain was causing a terror within me of what I was beginning to feel. I was scared, very scared. My mind was becoming aware of possible permanent ramifications. Then my mind was flooded with the memory of a book I had read thirty years before. It was a book about a man who had been in a car accident and his friend who was in the car with him had very serious injuries. They were both in the same hospital room. His friend was scheduled for surgery early the next morning; he had internal injuries. During the middle of the night, a bright light coming from his friend's bed awakened the man. He saw a giant hand come down from above and encircle his friend's body, squeezing, squeezing, as blood flowed onto the bandages. The man fell asleep, and when he awoke in the morning his friend was sitting up in bed, asking for breakfast.

The ride to the hospital was bumpy. When I arrived at the hospital I had the nurse call Barb, and Mark, my younger son. Mark was living in an apartment complex that belonged to our church, so an operator took his call. She located Mark, and even though I did not want him to come, he was on his way to the hospital. It still had not registered yet in my mind that I was not going to get up and walk away and drive my car home that evening, even though they told me at the accident site that my car was totaled. I told Mark not to come because I thought I would soon be out and on my way home. Once in the emergency room, an EKG was done. Then they took me to X-ray. The X-rays were very painful because of the angles they needed. I was still on the backboard; I was not to move my back or neck. It took a long time. I could sense that there was some internal bickering going on amongst the X-ray room staff, which did not make me feel very secure in what they were doing.

I was glad to see Mark. I felt heartsick when I saw the concern on his face. Then we had to wait for the X-ray results. It was decided I needed a cat scan of the neck and chest. The thought of being in that tube, even in as unaware state as I was, made me begin to feel like I was suffocating. I became terrified. The remembrance of the book I had read thirty years before again flooded back into my mind, lingering and staying. I felt the memory of it trying to soothe my fears to say to me that I'm going to be all right, there will be no serious injuries. This feeling stayed with me throughout the testing time and later on all throughout the next week. Sure enough, the tests did not show injuries that could be helped by any medical intervention. I was diagnosed with whiplash and soft-tissue injuries. When the doctor sat me up before I went home, the injured muscles, tendons, and ligaments in my neck and back began to throb. Unbelievable pain and weakness imploded throughout my whole body. My head felt like it weighed a ton. My body did not feel like it had the strength or energy to hold it up, let alone keep breathing with all of the pressure I felt on my shoulders, neck, and chest. Mark drove me home. I collapsed on my sofa. I could not move. He stayed with me that night. My church over-seer's wife, who was a nurse, had gone to the hospital but just missed me. She came to my house to check on me and make sure I took the correct medication dosage.

I guess I tried to play down what had happened, still not realizing the impact of it. I had always been very active, inde-pendent, and always doing something. Self-sufficiency had been my way of survival. This experience was the beginning of having to learn a new way. I called my boss that night leaving a voice message that I might be off for a few days. A few days, well, it was almost four months later before I could go back to work. Doctor visits were started immedi-ately and treatments with a physical therapist. In the begin-ning the therapists could not even work on me, the muscles were mush. I don't think it ever did register with me how much damage had been done to my body until about a year later. After I had begun to heal, I could tell how bad I had been. Because of this state of mind, I did not ask for help. I had never wanted to put anyone out because I had always been the giver. But it just did not register that I really needed help.

When I started back to work for three hours a day, I was in constant, horrible pain and wearing a neck support. It was a whole year before I could even stay up sitting in a chair that supported the back of my head until nine o'clock at night. I remember how happy I felt when I hit this point in my recovery. Then it began to dawn on me the actual physical limitations and pain that were now part of my life. I had so many new limitations. Being an avid exerciser and jogger, I could not even walk without pain. I did do exercises at the physical therapist's that helped strengthen my body. I was still in constant pain. I could not do normal daily things like vacuuming, lifting anything without pain, not even a small sack of groceries, or just daily normal things we have to do to get along. I gritted everything out, and took pain as a way of life. Since emotional pain was something I had my whole life, taking on this new physical pain only seemed natural, I guess. I moved into a tiny two-room apartment with hardwood floors so I had minimal cleaning to do. I stopped doing things with my friends, stopped involvement at my church, stopped my part-time jobs, stopped gardening, stopped doing everything in my life that was normal for me. Compared to the way I had been living, my "new" life was slow and heavy. It took a lot of energy to do anything, like walking from my car to the apartment. And if I chose to do something, I knew I would have to eliminate something else, or I would suffer more pain than normal for a week or so.

This lack of ability to have physical movement and endurance was limiting, plus all the pain. It all made me feel really old. With my background of living in a nursing home, which comes in a later chapter, to me "old" was equated with death. My thinking process began to change. Besides chronic pain, which normally causes depression, I would not admit to myself what the lack of freedom of movement was doing to my emotional state. One thing that kept my mind on a positive track was working with my children's books. I could sit in my chair exerting little energy and work on my books. I began to expand them. The little original world with three books began to explode, quickly growing to an imaginary neighborhood and twenty books, the number of characters growing at the same time. In this flow of working on my books, I found an inner energy and enthusiasm, as I would imagine seeing children's faces as they would hear or read these stories. I began to find a purpose in them, a purpose for my life of helping, of letting others know someone out there understands them, that they are not alone. Through a friend,

I met a small local publisher and worked with her. I began to learn about the publishing business and to rewrite. This was life-giving to me, and created a focus out there somewhere, maybe even just in a fantasy state at the time, but a focus beyond my limited daily life, the pain I had, and the lack of personal relationships.

Needless to say, after the accident, the physical pain, the lack of being able to do anything, complicated the emotional pain of missing Adam. The two seemed to play off each other. A level of hopelessness began to envelope me. It was similar to the hopelessness I had felt at a point in my marriage when I realized I was stuck in a desecrating relationship—but even in this I had my children as a catalyst that kept me moving, forging ahead. With Adam gone, with the pain, my children raised and on their own, I was encountering a loneliness deeper than anything I had ever known. I would not face the truth about my life and the circumstances of my life. I kept burying all these feelings, never dealing with them, never bringing anything to closure, and never moving on.

About two years after the accident, the depression kept growing, but I kept denying it because the other driver's insurance company was threatening me with insurance fraud. They said my medical bills were too high. Their assumptions, accusations, and lies propelled me into severe anxiety about my situation. Then I began to be sick all of the time, mostly sinus problems that would turn into flues or severe colds, even bronchitis. One day I had to be taken to the hospital from work by ambulance. I could not breathe, I felt numb, and thought I was having a heart attack. I lay in the emergency for eight hours as tests were done. Then a few months later, a cold developed into bronchitis and while coughing, my chest went into a spasm. I could not breathe and had another trip in an ambulance to the hospital. During the beginning of these illnesses, I was still being treated for the accident injuries, and my doctor kept asking me if I was depressed. I would say no, knowing full well that I would never want that to go into my medical record. It would be just the thing the insurance company was looking for; they had already distorted some of my past chiropractic and medical treatments, even for sore throats and such, trying to use these against me so they would not have to be responsible for a settlement. My healing was taking years and their medical bills and accountability kept rising. After the second trip by ambulance to the hospital, I knew I had to have help for the internal upheavals that continually overwhelmed my sense of being. I was anxious, afraid my heart would begin to race again, that my breathing would become difficult, that my next movement might somehow propel my body into the unreasoning fearful attack that I was going to die. My doctor prescribed a low dose of medication for me. It helped some, but I still felt anxious, and in constant fear that the attacks would come back. The only place I felt safe was in my house, sitting, not even moving in my house. I was my sole support. I had to work. It was three years of going through this trauma, after a lot of alternative type of treatments, that my doctor finally talked me into seeing a counselor, who turned out to be Miriam.

At about the time I began to see Miriam, I saw a program on public television that made me understand what was happening inside of my body. Post-traumatic stress disorder due to car accidents was something that had been studied extensively by two physicians at two major U.S. research hospitals. They found a way to use imaging technology that showed what was happening in the emotional part of the brain of a person who had been in a serious car accident. Between one and three years after the accident, post-traumatic stress disorder would set in. This was the body's normal flight-or-fight reaction. The trauma locked that part of the brain into constant triggering mode. Seeing this scientific explanation for what was happening inside of me was one of the most freeing experiences I had ever had. I knew now I was not a mental case and that no matter how hard I tried, controlling this was not within my own means, except by medication. Over these years I had people suggest this was happening to me because of my spiritual lack and my inability to control myself. This only made the attacks worse, and made me want to hide and withdraw more. This experience gave me a different, expanded perspective of the Scriptural verse that I think we have all heard from the time we have been small, "The truth shall set you free." I found the work of these doctors to be my freeing truth and I did not have to be ashamed any longer.

I had no idea at the time of the accident that the recovery process would be years in the making. After three years of living in that little two-room apartment, I had to get out. It felt like a prison in its smallness and limitations. A friend was renting a small quaint home. She had to move to Philadelphia for a season to assist her dying mother. She sublet the house to me, helping me cover the expense of the deposit since all of my money was now going for treatments and nutritional supplements. I could not wait to move in, to have no walls on the other side with noise from someone else, being able to really have my own atmosphere. I was also longing to garden again. Digging in the dirt and growing anything has always helped me to ground myself. It was always a spiritual experience for me as I watched the life growing new and fresh out of the earth. My first summer in the little house, I began to garden a few small spots along the side of the house. I would dig, work the soil, and plant for twenty minutes; then spend the next week or two in extreme pain. As soon as the pain subsided, I was back to digging. It was ever so gradual, but after three years of this process, I got to a point where I could work several hours in my garden without stopping. I felt life coming back into me.

Every summer our church has a large camp convocation. Church members from all around the world come. In 2004, the leaders invited ministries outside of our fellowship of churches to come and be part. Mahesh Chavda, an internationally known evangelist and healer, was one of those invited. He spoke during four services that year, and after each service would call people up for healing. On the first night, early in the healing service, he called up someone who had trauma from some kind of accident. I went up, overwhelmed inside with gratitude that there could be healing for me from this tortuous torment that medical science had no answer for yet, except to medicate. As I lay on the floor, slain in the Spirit as Dr. Chavda passed his hand from one head to the next, a healing process began inside of me. I could literally feel it. After a year I was able to get off the medication. I have also been faithful to research and work with my body to give it what it needs to be healthy. I found more alternative health practitioners that took my body to even deeper levels of healing, physically and emotionally. Sometimes healings come instantaneously, sometimes as a process, sometimes a combination.

I was thankful. During this time of living in the little house I worked intermittently on this book and my children's books. I changed jobs. My activity level increased. I started walking and am able to walk for a long period of time with no pain or after effect, no running yet though. Everything is rebuilding, slowly.

During this rebuilding time, the emptiness within me

is becoming less. I'm beginning to feel complete inside, all within my own being. I know that Adam was never my answer. Somewhere in the process of my body healing, my heart and soul have begun a process of healing. I stopped longing for him—even though I still missed the special attention. I started longing for my life to be everything it could be, for me to live the life I was intended to live.

PART THREE

MY EARLY LIFE

My intention here was not to go into all of the details or "normal" events of my daily life, but to give a synopsis of the highlights of memories that were the major factors through which I saw not only myself, but the whole world in relationship to me. When I was young I used to love to scrounge through the big box of family pictures that Mom kept in disarray. I loved looking at each person and at the places the pictures were taken. I remember big colored baby pictures of Patty and Jimmy, but none of me. In fact, there were no pictures of me until I was about a year and a half old, and then these were only a few snapshots from the side, so I never saw how I really looked. The next pictures of me were when I was between three and four. I loved to sort through the pictures over and over again. I think I was hoping I would find a lost picture of when I was a baby, wanting to find something about myself that I could connect to, to solidify my identity. I remember asking Mom where my baby pictures were, and she said there weren't any. I wondered why. Over and over and over again, I wondered why? Her answer left me empty; she just did not have any taken.

If we fast track forward from sifting through those pictures to forty-five years later, one day I received a small padded envelope in the mail. It came from my sister but was from my cousin living in Chicago. Uncle Ted had died several years before, which I had not known. His wife, whom he married after he and Aunt Jan divorced, found a small pile of snapshots that she had wanted to pass on to me. She did not know how to get in touch with me. I don't know how she knew that it was me in the pictures, along with Dad and some of Mom, since there was no writing on the back of them. It was a small stack of old snapshots that Uncle Ted had taken, and must have been right at the time Jimmy was born. I stared at the pictures, pouring over each one. They were all of me. I was able to make a connection of love for that little person in the pictures, a connection of the love that Uncle Ted had for me as he looked through the lens of that camera, wanting to hold me in the memory of his heart.

"Your mother hated you from the day you were born, Linda. I'm not sure why, but I think it is because you looked like her and she hated herself." It was another of Aunt Ruth's unusual phone calls, calling out of the blue with her bold shocking revelations every eight to ten years. Aunt Ruth and her twin Jan were Mom's sisters, born ten years younger than Mom. Aunt Ruth called me two weeks after my fifty-fifth birthday with this comment. I was living in the two-room apartment in 2002, still recovering from the car accident. This was not much of a birthday blessing. Aunt Ruth confirmed something I had felt my whole life, but could not prove, that indeed my mom did hate me from the time of my birth. I know she and Dad wanted a boy. All my sister and I can remember growing up is her talking about the son carrying on the family name and how she doted on my brother. So I was born new to this world, two years younger than my sister, Patty. I don't know how old I was when Mom began to go on her rampages and swearing fits. I can remember at a very young age of being left crying, neglected, being screamed and sworn at. Our home was this little trailer. At some point Dad had bought this silver trailer, maybe twenty feet long. He moved this trailer all over, with us in it. I can easily remember at least six different places in only two years.

He would just park it in someone's yard, and that would become home. Sometimes it did not feel like kids were too welcome in those yards though, so for me, no place felt like home.

Before I was three, Aunt Jan and Uncle Ted became extremely important in my life. They used to get me quite often to come and stay with them. She said they would get up in the middle of the night to check on me and find me "missing" only to be found sitting in one of their big rocking chairs, rocking. Uncle Ted bought me a very small stuffed rocker to sit in when I was at their home. When we moved away, the chair came with me because I remember sitting in it in the middle of the night way up until I was seven. The chair finally literally broke into pieces as the size and weight of my body overpowered its structure. After Mom died, Aunt Jan told me that Uncle Ted had wanted to adopt me. Something in me felt fulfilled when she said this. Mom died when I was thirty-one. Uncle Ted came to her funeral. I had not seen him for years, since I was in high school. I was so excited to see him, unsure of how to relate to him. When he walked into the front room, he came directly to me. I ran to him and we hugged. I glanced over at Dad and he was crying. Uncle Ted did not treat me special then. He and Aunt Jan had divorced around the time I was five. I don't remember him in my life much after that. But I do remember this deep longing and void wanting him to come back and take me to their home again, wanting to feel the safety of that love.

Mom put me in bed with Dad when I was about seventeen months old, right before my brother was born. I slept with him until I was about three and a half. Mom and Jimmy slept on the sofa- bed in the front room of the trailer. Patty slept in the alcove bed across from the "big" bed that Dad and I had,

I think it was an extra wide single or three-quarters. These were separated by the "hallway" or passage to the bathroom. The sexual abuse began during this time. What I remember is that I became special to Dad, his delight, so young, small, innocent. I blocked out the sexual part, even though it became play, and just longed for the attention, the times he would take me places with him. I remember my days, trying to avoid my mom in the cramped small trailer, wanting to not be a target of her hatred. Waiting, waiting until my dad came home so he would talk to me or draw pictures of rabbits, that I loved to have him do. I remember jumping into the middle of his lap when he would be trying to read the paper to get his attention, having already learned that part of the sexual play. But when he was home, I could sit, let my breath relax, and not be afraid for a while. But before he would come home, I never knew what was in store for me. Patty was often with her friends and then at school. Mom would decide that I needed my hair combed usually late in the afternoon, and set me up on a small, high, backless stool. I had very long hair. It was always matted together because I would sit for hours rocking back and forth on the sofa, batting my head against the back cushion, my hair becoming entangled in snarls. Mom would use a fine-tooth rat-tailed comb, and try to drag it through my hair. Of course it would get caught, then she would begin to jerk at the comb, trying to jerk it out of my hair. Not only did my scalp hurt from the jerks and the comb pulling the hairs, but also my whole head and neck would be jerked violently, almost causing me to fall off the stool. When I would cry, then the swearing and cursing would start, and the batting on the head. I had to sit still and not cry or else she would scream and hit more.

Dad would take me places with him. When I was three he worked for a logger for a summer and drove a small truck.

It was one of those old fashioned pickup trucks with the short wooden bed. I got to go with him in the afternoons and sit in the truck. Patty was in school, Jimmy with Mom. I loved the time away from the trailer. I was safe for a while with someone who would not scream at me. These times were a delight for me, away from the fighting and squabbling of Patty and Jimmy, away from the angry, seemingly vengeance that exuded from Mom. Sometimes Dad just liked to go places. He was more sociable when he was younger, but grew into a recluse as he aged. It was common for him to be off somewhere in the evenings or on weekends. Mom would want him to take one of the kids. She often suggested me and then it eventually turned out to be routine for him to choose me. It was fun, but Patty and Jimmy really resented me for this. And I saw and heard the disappointment in their faces and voices when they did not get to go. One snowy night the roads were slick. Dad and I were on our way to the movies. We had a minor car accident. I remember looking at Dad in the car behind the steering wheel, head falling forward, eyes closed. I cried as men from the gas station at the corner where we had the accident came and took me out of the car and into the station. I did not know what happened to Dad. When he walked into the gas station and took me I could not stop crying. I cried all the way as he carried me back to the trailer. Perhaps this bump on his head was the cause of how his behavior toward me changed. I don't know. I know that over the years I have heard of others who had received head injuries and their personalities changed after that.

Patty and I started getting locked out of the trailer when Jimmy was born. Maybe before but I can't remember that. It was, of course, always after Dad left for work. I was let in shortly before he came back home. Patty seemed to always get back in before I did. She ran somewhere with friends and left me to myself. I guess it was during this time I learned to listen to and watch the birds, listen to the rustle of the grass from the breeze, watch the insects in their busy ways with the flowers, watch the leaves fall from the tree and scatter along the ground, or watch the snowflakes fall gently and dazzle my mind with their intricacies. These are the things I learned to occupy my time with, the time that I had nowhere to go, no one to look after me, no food, no water, no bathroom facilities, for all day. As I said, Patty would often get back in before I did. When I would see this, I would try to get in also. Mom would hear me trying to come in the door, Patty would yell over at her, and Mom would scream to her that I could not get back in yet. Patty would then proceed to hang on the screen door of the trailer, and taunt me because I had to stay outside.

These times were difficult, being locked out, with no food, water, or bathroom facilities day after day. I can remember being out of energy and only being able to sit and wait. I remember being so thirsty I did not know what to do. I remember having to go to the bathroom so badly that my body was in wrenching pain and I would become almost ill and unable to move. When I was not allowed to go back in when Patty did, I did not understand. Often my heart would ache along with the rest of my skinny little body.

I don't know if it was the accident that changed Dad or the knowledge that perhaps he had been found out. It was an early spring day, maybe early April. The ground had a very light dusting of very wet snow that made everything seem very cold. Patty was off to school. A neighbor lady came over to visit with Mom. When she walked in, Mom shoved me out of the door—no coat, no shoes, no anything. It was cold for me. I could not leave the tiny porch because of the snow on the ground. Mom left the inside door open as she talked so I could have some heat from inside. She told the neighbor lady about Dad and me, about the sexual part of the relationship. I don't remember the exact words she used, but it was obvious her deep anger and resentment, and that she was accusing me, I was the guilty one, condemned. I will never forget the feeling as my heart sank. It felt like I had none left. I looked up at the trees and plopped down on the damp snowy step. I wanted to float up into the trees, to get away, to be away, forever. She kept talking, and I kept sinking, understanding the accusing tone of her voice and the way she was talking about me, but not understanding all of the words and what that all meant. I don't know how long I sat there. It could have been hours. I wanted to be nonexistent. The sleeping arrangements were changed. Patty and I were moved to the front room sofa-bed. Dad, Mom, and Jimmy all were now in the tiny hallway bedroom.

It was after this that Dad changed, but this was also close to the time of the accident. Mom would not let him take me any more, not to work, not to anywhere special. It was Jimmy now. Jimmy went everywhere with Dad. I just sat and dreaded each day. Dad also became very verbally abusive to me. The first time it happened we were at friends. He went into a swearing rage toward me when I asked to be set up on a tractor, like Jimmy had—Patty could climb up by herself. After his swearing fit and cursing at me, just like Mom always did, he put me on the tractor, but no one ever came to help me off. I can't express the emptiness of my heart. Everything was changed. I did not know what I had done to change it. He did not want to be bothered with me any more after work. His attitude and his demeanor seemed to be disgust toward me. As I grew older, it grew into an attitude of ridicule and criticism. This became my relationship with my dad. As hard as I tried, I could not please him and I began to feel awkward and uncomfortable around him, wanting to avoid him and be in a different part of the "house" when he got home.

When I was four, we sold the trailer. We moved into an old farmhouse owned by a neighbor where we had once parked the trailer. We drove through the night and ended up in the front yard of the old farmhouse. The car was crowded with all five of us. We had been traveling for hours, so it seemed to me anyway. Patty's and my bodies were scrunched so Jimmy could have room to stretch out. Jimmy was making terrible nasal noises that kept us from sleeping. Patty and I kept telling him to be quiet. The more we did, the more noises he made. Us kids were bickering while Mom and Dad were trying to tell us to sleep. Mom had had it—she made Dad, Patty, and me go into the old farmhouse to sleep on the floor. There were no lights inside, and we did not have a flashlight. We did have a couple of blankets that Dad spread down on the floor, right inside the back door. I pushed Patty over and told her she had to sleep in the middle. I had a creepy feeling and did not want to sleep next to Dad. I was afraid he would do something to me, to the private parts of my body, that I did not understand. I had to keep all of my fears hidden. I was forced to sleep between them and I stayed awake for a long time, tense, not moving. It must have been hours before I drifted off to sleep. This was the only remembrance for years of any strange sexual feeling with Dad, until I started into counseling in my mid-forties. Everything that had happened before I was four was buried and separated off into part of my being that I left alone and untouched.

The farmstead was very old. There was a hand pump in an old fashioned sink in the middle of a large barren kitchen. There was a small living room with a bedroom off to the side where Mom, Dad, and Jimmy slept. Patty and I had to sleep upstairs. It felt very spooky up there. I could never be up there by myself. I had become a nuisance that Patty had to put up with, so I was always at her mercy whenever I wanted to go upstairs. The electricity was skimpy, just a barren light bulb dangling from the center of the ceiling of each room. The house smelled of old wood dust. There was no inside plumbing of any kind. We had to use an outhouse out back. Dad got a job in town doing watch repair, something he had trained for on the GI bill after World War II. Mom and us kids stayed in the country during the day. Mom did not learn to drive until I was in junior high. The house was down a very long lane, far away from the road. There were big shade trees in the front yard and a huge orchard of large grown together fruit trees on one side toward the back of the lot. There was a large grassy area in front of the orchard. Behind the house was an old overgrown garden area with lots of old-fashioned flowers that had been reseeding themselves for years in the old plot and were also growing naturally alongside the perimeter of the fence. The whole yard had an old-fashioned wire fence around it. Everything was overgrown, even the tall grass that often went to seed. The countryside was beautiful. The house and yard sat on the top of a steep hillside pasture with a big stream flowing through at the bottom of the hill. Dad would take us down to the stream to play in the shallow parts while he fished and tried to net for minnows. This became quite a time of adventure.

The farmer that owned the land milked cows in the barn. The barn was off limits for us. The cows would run in the pasture where the stream was. Fred would come out during the day to milk the cows and do the chores. Mom still would chase us out of this big house, screaming at us to get out. It was not just because of the tiny trailer that she did not want us around. I vividly remember one particularly hot summer day. It must have been close to a hundred degrees. It was very, very dry. The sun was blistering. Jimmy, Patty, and I went out to play in the cool, almost chilling shade of the overgrown orchard. It seemed like a jungle as the branches of the trees all overarched into each other letting no sunshine through, no matter how intense the sun was. As had become normal, Patty and Jimmy ran off to someplace else, not letting me go with them. I was by myself. I imagine all of the times that I got to go special places with Dad made them do a special bonding to leave me out, as they must have felt left out as Dad and I did things together. They had always wanted to go with him too. The way I see it, Mom kept her two favorites at home, and she had Dad take me so she did not have to look at me or have me around, until she found out that is. Maybe.

Well this one particularly hot afternoon, about mid-afternoon I thought I would try to go into the house for a drink of the cool well water. The water was pumped directly from the well out of the old kitchen hand pump. I walked slowly up the back steps of the old porch. I crept across the porch to the door. Peeking in, I did not see Mom in the kitchen. The old screened door creaked as I slowly opened it, tiptoed inside, and timidly called out, "Mom." I dared not go in even to get a drink without asking her first, and I certainly could not reach nor had the strength to pump the handle. There was no response so I took a few cautious steps and called out a little louder, "Mom?" Then came the terrible shrieking, worse than I had ever heard before, so sudden, that I was terrified. It was not her normal yelling and swearing. The obscenities were worse, new words this time. The shrieking came from her and Dad's bedroom. She said I had better get back outside and not come any further, especially into the front room. She kept asking if I saw anything. I quickly ran outside and sat on the step. I wondered what had I done to create such a reaction. All I wanted was a glass of water. I was so hot and so thirsty. I sat on the step, hearing the ringing of the hateful voice in my head, more hateful than ever before.

I sat there and thought and thought. Then I made a plan. I walked from the front yard over to the taller grassy area on the side of the house. I found a spot where I could easily see the front door, but where the grass was tall enough so I could not be seen. The grass felt scratchy, was dry and prickly. I crowded down low to the ground and pulled the tall grass up around me, creating peepholes through the stems. There was no shade here. I heard Patty and Jimmy yelling for me from the back of the house. I stayed down, kept silent, as they walked through the yard looking for me, coming within about twenty feet of my hideaway. It seemed like I was there for hours. I was getting groggy, sleepy, thirstier. Then the creaking of the front door jarred me into wakefulness. As I peeked through the grass I saw him leaving the house, tucking in the front of his trousers with a smirk on his face. And I hated him. I did not understand what had happened, until I was much older and learned about sex. I had an innate sense that something was bad, and it involved the betrayal of my dad by my mom and his friend, Fred. Fred was about fifteen years older than Dad, dirty, sloppy, never shaven, smelling of cow manure, with a cigar always hanging out of his mouth, and always swearing and talking sexual nuances, even to me. Dad was vital, energetic, handsome, and winsome, with a medium build, exercising daily, light brown wavy hair and piercing blue eyes. I would often watch Mom and Fred flirting in front of Dad and Josephine, Fred's wife. The instantaneous hatred I felt for Fred and Mom in that moment turned part of me into an angry little girl. This was when my sympathy feelings for Dad started, feeling like I had to look after his feelings now. Strange how a child's mind tries to make sense out of things they have no control over and are not responsible for, forming belief systems that keep us locked for years into bondages and feelings that are not even ours. About fifteen minutes after Fred left the house, Mom called for us to come. I did not move. After Jimmy and Patty went in, Mom came out and called me by name. She wanted to give me some water. I stayed hidden for a long time yet, hoarding the anger and sense of betrayal for years to come.

When I was five we moved to Chicago, to the heart of the city where the row upon row of the old city homes rubbed shoulders with each other. We moved into Aunt Martha's basement. Aunt Martha was Mom's sister that was a few years younger than Mom. She was the one that Dad "fell in love with" when he saw her the day after he slept with Mom. Dad was on leave in Chicago during World War II. I don't know why he was in Chicago; his family was from the Midwest. He met Mom out drinking and dancing and they ended up in bed. The next morning Martha came home. She was younger than Mom, not burdened down with the responsibility of taking care of all the siblings like Mom was. She was thinner and very flirtatious with every man. I'm sure Dad married Mom out of the obligation of being with her. They married after knowing each other for a week. Then he shipped overseas for three years.

Even though my mom was not the smartest woman, she was sensitive and could sense the hidden passions between Martha and Dad, passions that stayed smoldering for years. So living in Martha's basement, with her and her daughters above us, did not make for a happier family. In fact, Mom did not want Dad to even talk to Martha. Mom became more bitter, more angry, as if that could have been possible. She hated Martha. The jealously was so obvious. She talked about it all the time when Dad was not around. We lived like this for four long years.

At Mom's funeral Dad brought out pictures of Martha when she was young, not of Mom, but of Martha. He displayed them so proudly to his brother—who was another relationship estranged through the years. Dad and his brother got quite drunk the day his brother arrived, the day after he, Aunt Jan, and I made the funeral arrangements together. Martha came to the funeral also. I had not seen her for at least sixteen years. She was still flirtatious with Dad. He had not seen her for at least twenty years. It was not too long before Dad moved to Chicago to live with Martha. I remember how shocked I was when this happened since Dad was always so discriminating about Patty and me dating. The years of hidden passion between him and Martha finally had expression only to realize that it was a fantasy. Dad died at age eighty-five, living fifteen more miserable years after Mom died. They were lonely and isolated years. My sister was with him when he died. I could not go. I did not want to see him. His body was cremated and I never saw him. Patty and I took his ashes in a cardboard box, dug a hole in the ground, and placed them in the ground beside our mom's body.

After leaving the house in the country and before moving to Aunt Martha's basement, we lived in a small mid-western community where Mom's grandmother lived. Maybe we were there for only six months; this is where I started my first few months of kindergarten. I do remember my great-grandmother. She was short, not much taller than I was at five years of age. She was tiny with a small round rosy face with wire rim glasses, and beautiful long white hair that rested in a bun, like a crown, on the top of her head. I was infatuated with her. She lived at the edge of town in an old farmhouse. The house appeared so worn from the years of weathering that it looked abandoned. I loved to visit her because she always lovingly hugged me. I was not used to that feeling much, but liked it. While she took Dad and Mom to the kitchen for coffee, Patty and Jimmy would play outside. She let me sit at her old-fashioned roll top desk in the large open hallway-entryway. The desk had lots of small cubbyholes and crevices to put things in. I could sit for hours enchanted with the maze of it all. I don't know why we left there and moved to Chicago. Probably watch repair work was more plentiful.

School was very traumatic for me. I had a lot of difficulty adjusting. I cried a lot and was sick a lot. I would not eat my lunches at school. I had trouble making friends. I was so painfully shy. I eventually did make friends and they became my sanctuaries. I was smart in school, very smart. Because I longed for freedom from my home life, I spent much of my after-school time studying, for hours on end. I found that this smartness, however, brought me attention that I did not know what to do with. It made me feel very uncomfortable. I did not want to be recognized for outdoing my classmates. I had already learned that for someone to be on top, others were on the bottom, feeling less. When I was in second grade I was the only child in all of the classes to get everything right in their spelling all throughout the year. My teacher made me take my spelling book down to the principal. He was a nice man, but I did not know what to say to him. The halls were crowded. I stood there for a long time not know-ing what to do. He finally saw me, and asked what I wanted. I handed him my book, not saying a word. I learned to not draw attention to myself because I did know how to behave when I had it. After this I would miss things on purpose so that I did not get special attention in class. Dad loved it that

I was smart—it almost became a bragging point for him. For a few years I relished in the fact that once again I found favor with Dad. But as I got older, into the fifth and sixth grades, still spending hours every evening studying, anywhere from two up to four hours, my attitude about liking Dad's attention for my brains turned into resentment. Patty and Jimmy did not try in school. They were not interested in school and had other things they preferred to do after school. They did average, sometimes even below average. It became common for Dad to criticize them for not getting the kind of grades that I did. I began to resent him because he took more pride in my grades than he did me. And I resented myself for being smart. I saw how it made Patty and Jimmy feel, to be put down and chided, not appreciated. Dad would pay me for my grades. If I got a B, it was not the praise I got for the A's, but why was there a B. When I finally rebelled against my dad in high school, I got back at him by becoming an average student. He could no longer lord my hours and hours of studying and my brains over my brother and sister. He could no longer make me feel like I was the cause of their seeming inadequacies, in his eyes anyway.

I learned that by my achieving, others were made smaller, were outdone, and felt less valuable. I saw these expressions in the faces of my sister, brother, and classmates as I was able to outdo them. All of this empathy, not wanting attention put on me, and learning to hide in closets for a feeling of security programmed me to want to just not be or do the best I could. I was not taught to stand in front of others and be proud of my accomplishments. The way Dad related to my intelligence really confused me. I felt pitted against my sister and brother. In a strange sense of protecting my inner self from all of these emotions, I wanted to hide my gifts and talents for fear of being different or taunted above others. I let myself settle into getting by, not just with my grades, but it transferred over to every area of my life. My life and career could have gone many directions. I had potential to be very successful, by the world's standards anyway.

Mom had become overweight. When she was younger she truly was beautiful. It was easy to see why Dad or any man would be attracted to her. In all of the pictures of her before she was married, she was always laughing and having fun. Aunt Ruth said when Mom and Dad were first married and Mom was pregnant with us, he would ridicule her and make fun of how fat she was. She said Dad was always making derogatory remarks, not only about her weight, but her intelligence, and virtually everything about her. It is no wonder that she grew bitter and hateful. I know she never talked back to him or stood up for herself. She went into a sad inner part and grumbled. There were a few times, as I got older, I walked into the house and found her crying. She would always deny anything being wrong. Her appetite became her means of consolation. She became quite overweight. Patty started gaining weight when she was about seven. Mom just let it happen. I remained normal sized. But this also became another issue for Dad to pit me against my family.

Mom dressed Patty like she was an old woman. She made her wear dark-colored, baggy long skirts and tops. I remember once when Patty was twelve, before she got her secret boyfriend, we went shopping to a larger city. Some young girls passed us. I could hear them giggling and realized they were making fun of Patty, specifically her clothes and hair. Mom ridiculed the girls. Inside I hoped Patty had not heard them. I also felt the pain of the hurt Patty must have felt. And again I felt ashamed for how I looked. Soon after this Patty got her secret boyfriend and started wearing brighter, more fun clothes, the kind a young girl should be wearing, started caring for her hair, and caring about how she looked. As a teenager she worked and bought her own clothes, and mine, until I got in high school and worked to do this for myself. She did not want me to wear the old-woman clothes Mom made her wear. Even though Patty resented me and was vocal about it, she wanted me to have nice clothes and not have the shame of what she went through. Maybe Mom saw the extra weight as a cover up for sexuality so was relieved when Patty started to gain weight.

After we became adults, Patty and I learned a lot more about Mom's life. It was not rosy. But the major impression for me was her contempt and shame about her own sexuality. Before Mom died she would tell us excerpts about her life when she was young and still living with her own parents, not good fun experiences, but things that still provoked much shame, anger, and resentment. There were two of Mom's stories that had a major impact in how I viewed her, especially in relationship to how she made me feel about myself. The first was when she was eleven. She grew up in the heart of Chicago, tall buildings, and crowded neighborhoods. Her older brother, two years older, was out playing with his friends on a Sunday afternoon and getting into things groups of kids should not be doing, but did. They were playing on location of a major high-rise building remodel. Billy fell. He died hours later in the hospital. According to Mom, her own mother said to her, "I wish that would have been you." Now whether this was true or whether it was something Mom created in her own mind due to the guilt of losing her brother, only God knows. The impact created something of her own lack of self-worth and her own self-loathing for the rest of her years. The second story that impacted me was about her as a young adult around eighteen, still living at home. Her parents were well into alcoholism by this time and out in the bars nightly, coming home and being abusive to all eight of their living children. Mom said she was ironing and her dad started toward her. I don't know if he was going to hit her or make sexual advances at her. Only my imagination was left to run the course because I never asked. Mom held up the hot iron to his face and said, "Come at me and you will get this in your face."

Around the time I was in junior high, Patty's weight had become a topic of confrontation in our house. Patty's and Mom's that is. The comparison of how Dad thought they should look was always directed at me. These discussions, which often turned into confrontations, left them with their faces turned downward, walking into other rooms, or Patty out the door to get away from the words. I was always aghast as I myself took on the hurt feelings and humiliation that I saw on their faces. These episodes always made me ashamed of how I looked. I would never ever in my wildest imagination ever want to compete with them, never want them to be criticized or harangued because they did not have the same size body I did. More and more I began to be in my room when I was home, hiding away. I can't imagine how much my sister and Mom must have resented me. It happened over and over again. I began to spend as much time at my friends' homes as I could, much like Patty had learned to do. I can't explain the strange humiliation I lived with because of how I looked. It was a sad, heartbreaking feeling of hurting two of the people that you want most in your life to love you.

Something strange that Mom and Dad would do while watching TV was always make fun of TV models, actresses, any beautiful woman in programs or commercials. We would all be sitting in the room and Mom and Dad would call these women names or ridicule what they were doing. Even beautiful women on the street or any woman that dressed well and took care of herself became a target for the taunting. I learned taking care of how I looked meant somehow I thought I was better than anyone else. Deep unconscious beliefs from listening to these chidings affected how I related to my body and my appearance for many years to come, accentuating the guilt, shame, and contempt already buried from the hidden sexual abuse.

After we moved to the Midwest, Dad would take the family fishing on occasional Sunday afternoons. Our favorite place to go was a lake about an hour drive from home. Dad parked the car by the dam and we would walk probably a half-mile to get to the fishing spot. This was a rough terrain and we had plenty of stuff to haul with us. When I was in the eighth grade, Dad, Mom, Jimmy and I went. Patty had opted out of any of these family outings by this time. A storm began to approach. It appeared dark and rather doomful to Dad. I had never seen him afraid of any weather before. Very suddenly, he decided it was time to leave, to try and stay in front of the storm. He was almost panicky. We picked everything up and trucked back to the car as fast as we could. He, however, was faster than all the rest of us and kept yelling back for us to hurry. At the car everything was hastily flung inside. We jumped into our normal seats. Dad was careless in trying to get the car out of the rough terrain. He got stuck in some ruts, unable to move backward. He took his revenge out on Mom. He made her get into the backseat, me in the front, yelling at her that her weight was too much in the front of the car and we could not get out. All the while she was trying to tell him she gets carsick in the back. He just became more disgusted. Even after he rocked the car out and drove away from the lake, well ahead of the storm, he would not stop the car for her to get into the front. I sat as though I was frozen in a lake of ice. My feelings, embarrassment, and humiliation for my mom made my whole body cold, not wanting to feel or think the thoughts I had. I felt it was not only more rejection of my mom by him, but putting me in a place where I had competed against her. I never went fishing with him again after that day.

Patty's whole life she always thought I was Dad's favorite. While from my perspective, my truth was that I only felt the effects of his critical words and strange controlling power the words had, a power that made me feel not only helpless, but less. In high school Patty had been very verbal about how she really felt. She saw me as the one that got all the looks, brains, and personality in the family. This competitiveness and jealously that was perpetuated through her eyes was expressed in her attitude and actions toward me. As the conversations about this surfaced in more recent years, I realized the deep resentment she carried. I also realized how I was continually trying to minimize myself to not be a competition to anyone, so others would accept me. She did not know what my life was like, on the inside, as I did not know hers. She only knew the façade that I put on for others. Things are not always what they seem to be—even to people living within the same family and household. What someone may perceive about another person is frequently misperceived facts or opinions, not the truth.

A few years before Dad died, Patty and I were having some discussions about our family and some of the feelings we had while growing up. This was long after Mom and Jimmy were gone. We talked about how Dad made us feel. She remembered him taking me places when we were little and, of course, the continual comparison of the grades. The weight issue never was spoken of between Patty and me. I know I did not have the courage to bring it up. Maybe she didn't either or just buried it to the point of no conscious remembrance, because that was one of his favorite criticisms for years back toward Mom. What we did talk about shed some light on more of my dad's strange behaviors toward us. For both of us, at the time when we began to develop physically, he would not look at us. When I would walk into a room where he was, or when I would talk to him, he would just look down at the floor, instead of at me. It was interesting hearing it from Patty, because I thought it was just me. I felt like by my body changing, I had somehow brought shame and disgust upon myself to the point that he could not look at me. How relieving it was to learn he had treated her the same way in this one area. She felt that shame too, but I know it affected each of us differently.

One holiday dinner after I was married and pregnant with my second child, I was sitting at my parents' dining room table. Jimmy and his wife, Jenny, Patty and her family, and Aunt Jan were all there with Mom and Dad. Dad probably had been nipping on the whiskey bottle because he was talkative. The more he would drink, the louder and more demeaning he would always become. Mom and Dad fought over his drinking from my earliest memories to the end. He did not run around with other women or even hang out in bars. But the contention became over the argumentative, derogatory remarks that never would die. They erupted like a suppressed volcano, spilling out on anyone who was near to listen. It was always after a certain point of his drinking that this was the course of events. After we kids were older, we learned to split, leaving Mom to sit and take the brunt of that viscous lashing-out. On this particular day he began to talk, as he so often did in the past, about how if he had it to do all over again he would never get married and never get tied down with the responsibility of a family. I had heard this statement from him many times since early childhood, usually while we were visiting with friends or family members. But this day the words struck me differently, maybe because I had my own children by then. The words stung deep into my being. I looked over at Mom as he said this, watching her face. I saw the years of hurt that had resulted in such deep bitterness and tiredness. I understood the words in a different way. Not only was this a verbal expression of his rejection toward her, but also toward all of his children. I was stunned. I realized for the first time how much Dad resented the responsibility of a family and the depth of being tied down that responsibility required of him. All of the burden I carried for him for years, of having a strange feeling of responsibility for his happiness, turned into resentment realizing he was saying none of us were really wanted by him and he lived in regret continually.

MY BROTHER

I don't know if I ever loved anyone more than my brother, except for my own children. We seemed to have a common understanding, a knowing of each other's feelings and thoughts. Jimmy was named James Jay after my dad's dad. He was eighteen months younger than I. The third-born child, after two girls, his birth was a time of cherished celebration for my parents—a celebration that I was not allowed to be a part of. I remember the day Jimmy was being brought home from the hospital. He was born in August so it was warm outside. Aunt Ruth stayed with Patty and me while Mom was in the hospital.

Patty and I were really excited about the homecoming—Mom coming home and seeing our new brother. Wow! My dad picked Mom and our new brother up from the hospital when Dad got off work. Arriving at the same time at our little trailer, in the trailer park, were their friends, Charles and Frances. Charles had polio as a child and was paralyzed. He got around with crutches and metal braces to support his legs. He had grown up with my dad as his best friend. They knew each other since they were ten years old.

When arrival time came, Patty and I were jumping with ecstatic excitement. We were quickly recognized as a noisy disturbance inside of the small trailer. We were ushered out the door, heard the door lock behind us, and were left shut out—out of all the happiness. All I wanted to do was see my new brother, who was he, what did he look like, what should I expect? I was eighteen months old—a year and a half. I sat on the step, and did not understand—I only wanted to see my brother. My sister, being all of three and a half, was much taller and wiser than I was. She ushered me around to the front of the trailer where the hitch was. She climbed up on the hitch and watched through the window, so excited by everything that was happening inside. She helped me to get up on the hitch, but I was too short to look into the window. She tried to boost me up so I could see. I could not get high enough. I could only listen to her report. She was happy to be a part by observing through this shutout window. I was happy to be part by observing through the eyes she provided for me. These eyes became a major factor in approving or, more often than not, disapproving of me regarding everything in my life for many years to come. This power that Patty had over me because I was smaller and younger became a relationship of bossing and overbearing for much of my life, as she became a verbal judge of what I did and was. Maybe in her eyes she was watching out for the little sister, and this was how it was done, learning from the examples we had.

It did not take long to realize that Jimmy was the apple of our mother's eye—her all-in-all, her reason for being. A boy, finally a boy to carry on our father's family name, a boy to make my dad's mother proud, a boy that was "the great desire" of my mom and dad. I loved Jimmy. There was something about him that became my purpose also. As time progressed, I learned what that was.

Mom used to talk about Jimmy like he was a saint. He grew to be an ornery and very mischievous child. Perhaps this was in part because he knew that no matter what he did, there were never any consequences he would be accountable for. He seemed to enjoy the rebuke others received as they happened to become entrapped in his schemes. Or maybe it was his way of coping with the conditions of our daily lives, the cursing, the strange relationship between him and Mom, and between him, Mom, and Dad. Jimmy always wanted to get someone into trouble, or hurt someone, so it seemed. He used to "hang" my dolls. Of course they were completely ruined in this process. I remember a specific time when I was trying to protect him. It was when we lived in the old downtown neighborhood in the center of Chicago. We lived across the street from a row of houses being torn down board by board. The whole area was piled with boards, all askew, with nails everywhere. For our play, some of the neighborhood kids would go and bounce on these boards. The ones that were stacked just so bounced like a diving board, low to the ground though. One day Jimmy and my bratty cousin were both there with me. Jimmy sat on one of the boards and my cousin began to bounce him as hard as she could. It was easy to see that if he fell, he would fall right onto some of the large protruding nails. I screamed at her to stop. The more I did, the harder she bounced. After my voice became hoarse, I finally swore at her. She stopped dead in her actions. My brother marched right over to our house. He told my dad I had sworn, even though he knew I was trying to protect him. He saw a chance to get someone into trouble. It was a beautiful Sunday morning and I had to sit inside until I said I was sorry. I sat there all day with no food or water, even though Mom snuck some to me when Dad stepped out of the apartment. I even had to ask for permission to go to the bathroom. I was finally allowed to go to bed very late when I could not keep sitting up any longer. I never apologized. That was not because I was a brat, but because I felt an internal integrity to protect Jimmy, which I had done. Jimmy was smart, very spoiled, and knew how to play Mom and Dad to manipulate everything that he wanted.

Jimmy was a natural schemer to also cause havoc in the family. One of these methods was his decision to not eat. Meals at our house were a time of trauma. Mom would loudly and angrily complain in the kitchen, banging pans, tossing utensils and dishes, cursing because she had to prepare a meal. Her meals were always cooked fast without any thought given to the nutritional value or appearance of the food presented to us. Mom then yelled at everyone to come and eat. Jimmy always decided not to eat. Mealtime was horrible, a time of contention, fighting to make Jimmy eat. Jimmy would be obstinate. Mom would curse. Dad would be quiet and eat quickly so he could leave the room quickly. I always pretended I was busy and waited until everyone was gone from the table before I would go into the kitchen. Jimmy was usually the only one left at the table by the time I got there. He would stay and mess up the table as much as he could, after causing all the havoc. There was not much food left by the time I sat down. If there was food left, I had no appetite remaining after listening to all of the angry words. I would just pick at the food. No one ever noticed what I ate or did not eat. I was unnoticed, nice, quiet, little Linda—skinny, often running out of energy, and sad, deep inside. My sister did just the opposite, as she would overeat. I'm sure it was an avenue of finding love, acceptance, and consolation.

Eventually, to get Jimmy to eat, no matter what Mom fixed for the family, she had to fix Jimmy a hamburger on a bun, and corn, any kind of corn. Except for breakfast, these became the only foods he would eat. I know it was his way of not only causing havoc and getting attention, but a round-about way of making himself feel special. I don't think any of us could have felt special. How could we? I only know how I reacted inside to the words, the screams, the cursing, day after day. I don't know what happened inside the heads and hearts of my sister and brother as they heard the same words.

When I was in third grade Mom had a gall bladder operation. We were living in Chicago in the basement apartment. Jimmy and I had to go and stay with Aunt Jan. She, her second husband, and baby daughter, Alice, lived all the way across the city. Patty got to stay home because she was supposed to be helping Mom. It was a horrible two weeks. Aunt Jan had one of those personalities that said you could do one thing one minute, while the next was screaming at you for doing the thing she just told you it was okay to do. Alice was not quite a year old and she used to beat her because Alice would cry when put in bed for naps or nighttime. Jan would freak out and beat the child, frantic in her behavior. Mealtimes at her house became more of a torment for me than what our meals were at home. Jan's husband decided that he would make Jimmy eat the food that was in front of him. I cringed inside and became sick watching this day after day, meal after meal, the arguing and contention as he tried to force the food into Jimmy's mouth. Many harsh and unloving words were angrily spoken as it became a battle of wills. The harsh attitude made Jimmy even more determined to not eat. I grieved even more as I saw his poor spirit grow more wounded and broken, as he would break into tears, agonized and angry.

I'm not sure at exactly what age it began to be apparent that, for some reason, Jimmy was not growing as normal kids—kids his age, kids in his class. At first he just looked skinny. By the time he was in third grade, it was more obvious. By the time he was in high school his body stopped growing, maintaining the look of a skinny, small-boned boy, reaching a height of five feet, six inches and never getting above one hundred and ten pounds. Muscles and the normal masculine shape that young men acquire as they mature never happened in Jimmy's body. However, other parts of him kept maturing, rapidly. His skin became thin and patchy. His hair became stringy and brittle. As the years progressed, his eyes took on the look of empty despair and bewilderment. At age twenty-five he had the body of an eighty-five-year-old man, as diagnosed by doctors at a major research hospital. Why hadn't my parents tried to find help for him when he was much younger? Only God knows. Perhaps there were hidden thoughts deep within their own minds that wanted to keep Jimmy all to themselves, locked into a dependence on them, a place of retreat in their home. Or, maybe it was guilt for how he grew, guilt that they could not face. It was at Jimmy's desire to try to find answers to his life that he finally did get this diagnosis. It confirmed to him what he already knew about himself—he was old beyond his years, with no provision to change, no chance of restoration. He felt hopeless and tired. The rest of his life was given to alcohol, drugs, and futility—only to end in sudden death four days after his twenty-ninth birthday.

The years of growing up and watching Jimmy, listening to him, being badgered by him, but eventually being invited to share and become part of his inner thoughts, fears, and world, were grievous for me. He often played by himself. When I lived in the attic of the nursing home, between the cabin and nursing home there was a good size patch of dirt, maybe fifteen by twenty feet. Jimmy "owned part of this dirt." He would spend countless hours mounding the dirt and playing with his little plastic army men, one major war after another. I owned the other part of the dirt patch. We actually called this dirt patch a garden, which was a misnomer even with every stretch of the imagination. The first part of my dirt patch was my "garden" area. I consistently was trying to raise some kind of vegetable or beautiful flower year after year, all to no avail in dirt long dead. Another major factor in this failure was the fact that I did not even know how to garden. The second part of my dirt patch was my burial ground for all of my animals. I had to have a burial ceremony and plot for them.

Jimmy was frequently in his dirt patch, since it was his only place to be by himself. He had to sleep in the cabin bedroom with Mom and Dad until he was ten. I would walk by him playing in the dirt mound, going between the nursing home and the cabin, engrossed in making his war sounds. I don't know what kinds of things he did with his friends, but he was often alone. I always felt sad inside when I saw him playing by himself. Maybe I was feeling something in his heart that he never let show. He became Dad's best fishing and hunting buddy. They were always running off together most weekends to some place where life had a different meaning. He did have a few friends who stayed close to him, and for them I was thankful. When it came time for dating and girls, of course he was left out. His friends became the other young outcasts who were different from everyone else in some way. For all of them, their best friends became alcohol, then drugs as he became an adult—the ultimate escape from everyday reality.

When Jimmy was ten and I was twelve, we became friends. We were living in our first "real" home, having just moved from the nursing home into a house. All three of us kids got our own rooms that became our private venues to retreat to. Mom even made our evening meals. She was still grumpy through the process, but at least the swearing and cursing were not verbally spoken any longer. This was like a dream come true for me, our own home, all of us together under one roof and living like a "real" family. We could have meals together and share the same living room. We even had our own yard with fruit trees. Mom got into doing some homey things and I got to help her. I got to help pick out curtains and helped her make some drapes. I felt camaraderie with her for the first time in my life, like we cared about how we were living our lives. Perhaps it was this major change in our home environment that provided the real opportunity for Jimmy and me to spend time together in the living room, alone. Since Patty was always gone, and Mom and Dad would go to bed early, Jimmy and I were left together in the living room, just the two of us. Unlike the nursing home, in this new house I could stay up in the family arena without being shoved off to my attic room. Jimmy and I spent many hours together in these late evenings. My parents did not pay much attention to the time we finally did get to bed. Jimmy and I found a refuge in the silly things we found pleasure in.

Jimmy's room was downstairs. Patty's and my rooms were upstairs. This was the first time Jimmy had separate sleeping quarters from Mom and Dad. His room was mounded with his toys and comic books. He often locked himself inside this boxed-in room. He kept it strictly off-limits to the rest of us. He read comic books continuously. His imagination was where he lived. Every Saturday night Jimmy and I would stay up as late as our eyes could remain open. We loved to watch old "Andy Hardy" movies and any other old funny or scary movies we could find on the channels. We anticipated these times all throughout the week. We spent the time laughing and laughing, like our insides were so tickled. This was before the days of satellite, cable, and dish. We only had a little antenna for reception in a somewhat snowy black and white screen. Jimmy was sensitive toward me. I felt it. I felt the same toward him. He began to talk about dreams that scared him, or feelings that scared him. I would listen and try to help him, with my extra eighteen months of life experiences already behind me. One of these dreams I remembered years later, it was one that he had into his adulthood. After he died, the memory of him telling me about this came back to me. He was trapped in a room and could not find the doors and windows to get out. He was afraid inside of that room, like there were spooky things in there that would try to destroy him. I realized that the room he was trapped in was his own life, his own body, and he could not escape the horror of how he viewed himself.

It was this special bonding that created a place of respect and unique love that has never died in my heart, even when Jimmy did. We carried this late Saturday night practice of watching crazy or scary movies on throughout high school. Frequently on weekends with Patty included now, the three of us would stay up late into the night. More often than not, we found ourselves laughing and talking, not paying any attention to the movies that we used as our excuse for this special time. Patty and I would often make our favorite cookies, or we would have friends join us.

Jimmy was very intelligent, but Dad would not let him go to college. He did not study nor try to get good grades in school. He did average. He took to working in details with his hands. This was something that was easy for him to do. It required little physical effort. He had incredible eye-hand coordination. When he was in high school he took up taxidermy. It was not only something to do with some of the little animals that he and Dad shot, but it became a time-consuming hobby. It kept him shut up in his room, away from everyone, including the world. He became bitter during this time, and more withdrawn. Our friendship was waning. I began to spend most of my time with my one best friend. She and I chased around with boys. Jimmy was drinking heavily, every day. This was something that I learned from him many years later. He daily drank from a fifth kept in his bedroom. Jimmy also became good at drafting. So when he graduated from high school, Dad forced him to get a job as a draftsman in a city ninety miles away. He forced him out of the house. I was stunned at how Dad did this. Jimmy was not ready and not prepared to be out on his own. My sister and I bought his clothes and went to visit him often. He was becoming more and more anti-social.

When I was nineteen we moved to another town. My parents bought a different nursing home. Jimmy moved back home after he quit his job in the city. I had married a farmer. Jimmy would come out and help on the farm. I loved it because I could feed him. I kept thinking a miracle might happen and he might grow and fatten up a little. And we would talk. He even worked as a hired hand for our neighbor for over a year.

One of the things that we talked about while he was coming to the farm was his beginning interest in drugs. He thought about it long and hard before he started on the drugs. He wanted my input. This was the time when LSD was becoming popular. I remember buying a book entitled *LSD and the Search for God*. It was my effort to try to get some insight into how I could give Jimmy just the right input so he would not get into the drugs. I could not understand from his point of view that by this time he already viewed his life as hopeless and futile. He eventually ran off with some of his high school friends who did drugs and took off around the country. He settled in Omaha where my sister and her husband had settled. Jimmy of course kept on with the drugs, finding new friends in that world and selling drugs. He told me of some of his experiences and stories. They were quite terrifying. One of his roommates was Jenny, an abused and wild gal that became pregnant by the other roommate, who deserted her. Jimmy stayed with her and helped her through the pregnancy. She gave the baby up for adoption and married Jimmy. They both moved back home with Mom and Dad. I had not seen Jimmy for a year, perhaps, when he moved back. I drove in the long driveway, up to the back of the stately nursing home where Mom and Dad lived in an attached cottage-type house. I was nervous in anticipating seeing him again. I was shocked to see that he had become a skeleton, maybe eighty-five pounds, with straggly beard and hair, and browning splotched skin. I noticed how his eyes appeared bulging and glazed, seemingly full of the desire to hide, continuously averted to objects beyond the glance of those around him. I had wondered if he saw the shock, dismay, and sympathy in my own eyes when I saw the demise of his body. And if he did, perhaps that made him feel more shame in how he looked now, so defeated, so hopeless.

Jenny was jealous of Jimmy's and my relationship. She is the one who told me how highly he valued me. They were together for the next four years until he died.

I don't know how I can express the sensitivity I had toward Jimmy, or the sorrow in my heart I carried for him for the way he felt about himself. It hurt to watch him in school, with his friends, at school functions, watch that little person who longed to be like everyone else, not even handsome, athletic, or popular, but just desiring to be normal. I think I carried this pain in my heart, and never showed it outwardly. Except I know Jimmy felt it. He felt the compassion I had in my heart for him. I'm sure this is why he would open up and trust me. I wanted to change his whole life. I prayed and prayed for years and years for him to grow to be normal. When I became interested in nutrition and health food, I tried to get him interested in it too. He took a turn to try to build his health. He would backpack up and down the ravine in Mom and Dad's back yard trying to build up his muscles. He would eat the concoctions I told him about to try to put some super nutrition into his body. It was at this time he decided to go to the hospital for testing. He hoped they would have an answer to help him grow and develop, even though he was now an adult.

I remember a dental appointment Jimmy had. He was probably about twenty-two. We were all living within a radius of about twenty miles at the time. It was before Patty moved to Omaha. Jimmy was living with Mom and Dad, before he took off around the country. Patty and I drove with him so we could shop while he was at the dentist. We were gone for a while thinking we would give him ample time to do what needed to be done. When we came back, Jimmy was ready. He was very quiet when he got into the car. We finally started asking him what they did, and if his mouth hurt. He was very sullen and quiet. He just shook his head and said the dentist told him his mouth was too small, it would not open wide enough to get the tools in to do what needed to be done, just to use salt water to try to alleviate the pain. I felt a deep sense of guilt, hurt, and sadness go throughout my whole being—guilt that I looked "normal," hurt for his feelings in how this dentist treated him, and sadness. Something inside of me knew then his only answer out of the agony of his life was death.

I remember once when Patty and I were having babies, her third and my second, I had said something to Jimmy and Jenny about having babies. He just had this far away look in his eyes, not connecting to anything I said. Later Jenny told me he did not want to have any children. He was afraid they would look like him. My heart cried inside. I would have loved for nothing more than for Jimmy and Jenny to have a child, to have another part of him to share in my life.

Two weeks before his twenty-ninth birthday, Jimmy and Jenny had moved to the northern part of the state where my sister had moved a few years before. They were staying with her until they found a place of their own. They often stayed up late playing cards or games. One night, while they were playing cards, Jimmy was doodling on some scratch papers. The next morning he did not feel right. Patty had gone off to work. Jimmy walked around the house for a time, maybe an hour. Jenny knew something was really wrong. She called Patty from work. Jimmy sat down in the chair he had played cards in the night before. He looked up and said, "I can't hold on any longer." Then he fell out of the chair onto the floor. He was gone. Patty arrived within five minutes. Since Patty was a nurse she began to administer CPR. It was too late. She told me about his facial expression, how his eyes were fixed and gazing out straight. We both loved him and wanted to protect him from everything. Now here he was, gone without a word, without a goodbye. Patty called me to tell me. I lived a three-hour drive away. As I heard the words, thinking it was going to be about Mom, I screamed and began to bang my head onto the floor. The hysteria lasted for about a half hour before I could let the words bear their truth into my heart, my being. I heard Jimmy's voice as I tried to get a grip of this new reality, "I am happy, and I've never been happy before."

That night of Jimmy's death, I lay on my sister's sofa trying to sleep. I felt betrayed by the loss of someone who was so dear. Suddenly, gently, I became aware of another presence in the adjoining dining room. It was Jimmy. However, this was not the defeated, shriveled person who was entrapped within the body, but a glowing, vibrant, joyful and peaceful spirit, free and happy. He did not show up at this time for me. He walked into the room where his wife and my cousin, Alice, were sleeping. I finally drifted off to sleep. The next morning I kept quiet. I learned at a very young age that any conversations about the Lord or the Spirit in my family, except with Jimmy, were not only not welcomed, they were ridiculed and shamed. It was that afternoon, after we had made some funeral arrangements, that Alice, Jenny, and I were together without my sister. They began to talk about what they experienced the night before, for the first time between each other. At the same time I became aware of Jimmy walking into their room, they both saw his shadow appear on the wall. A streetlight was shining into the window and a shadow was cast on the wall opposite this window. Jimmy turned as his spirit entered the doorway so they saw his profile. They both immediately recognized the contour of his uniquely shaped nose. He turned his head upward, brought his hands together in front of him, the form that we see in many pictures of people who are in reverent prayer and stayed in that position for a few seconds. Then he was gone. Jenny and Alice were too scared to talk to each other about it that night. Jimmy left them a valuable message.

On the kitchen table, in front of the chair where Jimmy sat and doodled the night before he died, the chair he had died in, Patty caught a glimpse of the doodles on the notepad. There were numerous ones, but the one that we all took notice of was one of a guy with horns, like a devil, and an arrow attached with the words, "James, I." These were the eyes Jimmy saw himself through all throughout his life. Dad took great care that his son would never grow up to be a believer. Jimmy could never get free from seeing himself not only through his own hatred of how he looked, but the haunting thoughts that his existence might not have been of God.

I do know one thing. Before Jimmy moved this last time, he found a friend, somehow through that myriad of drug related subculture and inter-relationships, someone who did lead him to Jesus. Jimmy and Jenny stopped over to the farm one evening, unexpectedly. As usual, my husband was busy with farm work. I tried to talk to Jimmy as much as I could. I walked them out to the car. After his wife was in the car, before he opened his door, he told me he had received Jesus. He gave me a knowing look, like now he understands what I was trying to tell him. It was a few months later that he died.

A couple of years after Jimmy died our church was having a baptismal ceremony. My husband, children, and I had been going to this "new" church for about two years. I had been baptized as a child in the Lutheran church in Chicago. We never went to church when I was small. I remember going once when I was five. I can honestly say I did not even know what it meant when Mom had the three of us baptized. I think I was seven. Mom had our neighbor, Mrs. Johnson, be our "godmother," whatever that meant. All I remember is that Patty, Jimmy, and I all stood there, not understanding a thing the pastor said as he read, dribbling this water over us. We were laughing and bursting inside with fun, while Mrs. Johnson and Mom were weeping. Of course, as an adult, I learned what baptism meant. When our church was offering this experience to those who had not been baptized by immersion, I realized that I needed to experience this. My whole family was baptized at the same time. My sons were eight and six at the time. My husband was mad at me about something, as usual. I was always on edge, nervous, never knowing when he would erupt into his unreasonable anger at something I might have said or done, or not said or done. Some visiting ministries came to our church to do the baptism with some of the local ministries. When it came my turn, the lead ministry looked at me and said, "You have another child." I abruptly said no. But he persisted. After about his fourth time of saying this, and mentioning that it was an older child, I became extremely uncomfortable wanting him to stop because I was afraid my husband would accuse me of having a child before we got married. His mind worked overtime to find things to accuse me of. The minister finally said, "Well, maybe not a child, but someone close, like a brother." And immediately, I knew he was talking about Jimmy. As the minister stood there and looked at me, he went on and said, "You had to watch him suffer so you could learn compassion. He is still with you."

I had to wait until I was alone, away from my husband, before I could cry. It was hard for me to cry about Jimmy, because after I started, it was hard to stop. This experience made me feel guilty, like I was some kind of horrible person, and Jimmy had to suffer so greatly in this life to teach me something. But as I have matured over the years and learned more of the real God, not the mean guy that is there to punish us and tell us how bad we are—but the Father who loves and has great compassion for us—and experiencing His great love for myself, I realized that I would not be who I am today and I would not be writing this book if it was not for Jimmy. He taught me to look at others with a heart that wanted them to be touched to feel good about who they are, wanting them to be whole and healed—that they are valuable and deserve to feel valuable and loved. If this book touches one person in that way, as his life did mine, his suffering had purpose and can make a positive impact in the earth. And I realize that by sharing my story, I am sharing his.

LIVING IN THE NURSING HOME

I was eight years old and going into the third grade when my life became entwined with something that was not even imaginable. It was late summer. At night we loaded up the car with all of our belongings and drove out of the center of Chicago. Uncle Ted had come over and helped us load everything. He basically was not our uncle any longer since he and Aunt Jan had divorced. We never saw him for visits any more. He followed us through the city and onto the freeway, honking and waving as he passed us one last time to say good-bye. We were on our way to a new state. We had lived in this state for about six months when I was five and I started kindergarten there. But this time we were going to a different small Midwestern town where my Grandma Josephine, Dad's mom, owned and operated a nursing home. She also owned a nursing home sixty miles from where she lived. She was giving the second nursing home to my mom and dad for their livelihood. Dad had been working in Chicago as a watch repairman and Mom was working the graveyard shift cleaning at the university. Besides living in an unsafe neighborhood, Dad could not provide the financial security a family of five needed. We were still living in the basement of Aunt Martha's going on four years. Dad's mom came to his rescue, as she always came to the rescue of her two sons, no matter what it was they needed rescued from. This rescue became a major nightmare in my life.

We arrived at Grandma Josephine's place in the middle of the night. We were put into rooms in the upper floor of the nursing home. The nursing home had originally been a very large family home, numerous rooms off of hallways that one could almost imagine to have been a small hotel at one time. My sister and I were left in a room together. Grandma had done the best she could to make it feel like a real room, beds for my sister and me, and nice bedspreads. When Dad put us in bed, he said where Mom, Jimmy, and he would be, but it did not register with me. When I awoke the next morning, my sister was already gone. I had no idea where my family was. I opened the door of the bedroom. All I saw were hallways and rooms. I walked into the hallway only to be entreated with a most grotesque odor that irritated my nose and made me nauseous. Later, as I began to learn about the nursing home, I realized it was the combination of compounded urine and bodily decay masked over with a pungent eye-stinging disinfectant cleaner. I walked by two of the other rooms. As I peeked inside the door, I saw old worn-out looking people lying in high metal beds. The people were starring at the ceilings, covered up to the neck with white sheets, in the white rooms. Some of the people were sitting in chairs, staring straight ahead. The odor reeked out of the rooms and into the hallways. Some of the rooms emitted sounds of groaning and breathlessness, sounds that were not of ecstasy, but of suffering. I had never seen old people whose bodies were broken and helpless. I quickly retreated back into "my room," hoping that the door I choose was the right one. I sat on the bed. I looked out the small dirty window, which was at floor-level. The sun was out bright. The outside looked inviting. I just did not know how to get out there.

It seemed like I sat on the bed for hours, looking out the window. Finally, Dad knocked at the door and peeked his head in. He asked why I had not come down. I went with him, dragging slowly behind as he walked briskly through the house. He seemed to know where to turn, where to go down a stairway, which doors to go through. I was lost. We entered a cramped kitchen that was full of women flurrying around everywhere. Some were cooks. Some were nurses. All were dressed in white uniforms and were busy. Then we went into the "front" room. There was Mom and Grandma. Mom was dressed in the white too. She did not acknowledge me when she saw me. Jimmy and Patty were outside with my cousin. I don't remember what happened next. I only remember the overpowering odors coming from all of the adjoining rooms, of peeking into the rooms and seeing the bodies laying in strange positions, all with that same groaning of suffering.

During this time, Mom was supposed to learn how to run the nursing home. I don't know about Dad, but when we finally did move, he went back into watch repair. This was a time of great insecurity for me. I never knew where to find Mom, Dad, Jimmy, or Patty. This was a time when the relationship between Mom and Dad really began to show its colors. It was not uncommon for me to find Dad in the kitchen, talking and laughing with the nurses. He would drink a special mineral water that he had gotten from a spring, all the while teasing how it would make him young. The women loved to talk and laugh with him. This behavior made me feel very uncomfortable. I noticed a look in everyone's eyes. (I could faintly remember seeing this look in Mom's eyes as she used to talk with Fred.) Whenever this was happening, Dad never even noticed I was around. And it made Mom furious. I began to feel sorry for Mom, unconsciously picking up the sense of betrayal that was so subtly happening in the relating, even though no real affairs happened that I could be aware of anyway. Plus, on top of that, my cousin, Harvey, who was a year older than my sister, lived with Grandma. Harvey was unruly and mean. I lived in constant fear of him. One day when I was hiding in my "room," Harvey stuck his head in the door and asked me a weird question. I did not understand exactly what he meant, but it seemed like it might be sexual. I had an innate sense that I should never be alone with him. The only safe spot I found was sitting on the back step, right outside the kitchen. The drone of the women in the kitchen was in the background and the lovely sounds of the birds in the big shade trees of the back yard were in my foreground. I sat there for hours, alone, except for a friendly tom cat that used to come up to be petted. I would sit for hours and talk to him. Then one day the cat did not come. Not the next, either. Dad started looking for the cat. Harvey had hung it by the neck in the shed about thirty feet from the back door of the kitchen. My only refuge from this existence was now gone.

I was not the only person Harvey tormented. He tormented my sister and brother too. My sister was in fifth grade at this time and beginning to develop, plus being overweight. Harvey hit her in the belly several times. Unfortunately he seemed to take pleasure in this act. Jimmy, so small yet mouthy, was a great target for Harvey just to taunt and bat about the head. One day we all gathered on the back steps. Patty and Jimmy were telling on Harvey, for I don't know how many times. No one could cross Harvey since he was Grandma's special baby. Dad got fed up. He called Harvey over to where we were. He started punching him in the belly and hitting him and asked how it felt. This was one of the times that I thought Dad did love us. Patty, Jimmy, and I just stood there and chuckled to each other in delight to see this. I know Grandma was not too happy. We were gone soon after this.

I also started third grade there. It was awful. My teacher was newly out of college. She was quiet and could not keep control of the class. The class was chaos. I was so quiet and so out of my element without a solid home or family life, the classroom became an extreme time of trauma for me. I finally started crying in class one day and could not stop. After that I would walk to school in the morning, get to a certain point, and then just stop. Often I would either go back home and pretend I was sick or just walk around all day. Luckily we were there for only six weeks of the school year.

Needless to say, time to move could not come soon enough for me. One day we were up and gone again—the same pattern Dad always had. He always seemed restless and made impromptu life changes without thinking of the consequences. This time though we did have a place to go to— the nursing home that Grandma was giving to my parents. To top this off, Mom and Dad were the owners. I knew this meant something of significance, but without understanding the impact of it.

Our new nursing home at one time had been quite a stately home. It had a formal parlor with fireplace, beautiful woodwork throughout, an open winding stairway, servant stairs from the kitchen to the upstairs, and a full attic. To meet state safety codes, the open winding stairs had been enclosed. The beauty of the home had been overcome with the nursing home look and odor. Each of the large stately rooms had three to four beds, either lined up like in a barracks, or lined around the perimeter of the room. The beds were intermittent with chests, dressers, tray tables, and padded sitting chairs framed in metal. There was one bathroom on the first floor with a shower. It was located off the old original dining room that had been made into a sitting room. This sitting room had a TV and two plastic overstuffed rockers, one pale gold, one pale lime green, with a couple of tables and lamps. The sitting room was austere. There was one bathroom on the second floor. This at one time was probably a linen closet. It had a bathtub, but no shower. In the attic, there were no bathroom facilities. There was a shower in the basement. The home sat on a corner lot with large elm trees giving ample shade and structure to minimize the size of the home. Behind the nursing home was a small cabin with two rooms. The cabin had no bathroom or kitchen facilities, just a living room and bedroom separated by a wide arch and a curtain. The cabin sat between the alley and nursing home and next to the large combination driveway-parking lot.

I remember vividly the first night. We arrived close to midnight. My sister and I were to sleep in the attic of the nursing home. There were two empty rooms up there that would become ours. The third room housed a young woman by the name of Dorothy. She had fallen from a haymow door when she was a child and had permanent brain injuries. Dorothy did all of the dishes for the nursing home. There were no automatic dishwashers quite yet. She kept the kitchen clean. It was her domain. She was also very grumpy and aggravated by children. We soon proved to be an annoyance to her. Dad took Patty and me to the attic. The doorway to the attic was at the top of the beautiful wide staircase in the front of the nursing home. Inside the attic door was a smaller narrow stairway going up into a larger central room encircled by three doors to the bedrooms. The lights in the attic were burned out, except for Dorothy's room. Dad had a flashlight and he left us there, on mattresses in the central room until our rooms could be furnished. The smell of the attic was dusty, like wood dust that had been enclosed in a dry room for years and years. He left a crack in the door at the bottom of the stairs so a little light could come up. After he left, my sister quickly fell asleep, or at least pretended she did so she did not have to listen to me. I crawled over to the top of the stairs, clinging to the light that came up. It was a dangerous place to sleep because there were only two horizontal railings around the stairway, no vertical banisters. I could have easily rolled under one of the railings. I did not care. I needed to see the light. If I crawled a little further over, there was a window at the top of the stairway from which I could see the cabin in the back. I watched Dad go into the cabin, knowing he and Mom and Jimmy would be in there. I wanted to be there too.

I don't remember any of the details of those days immediately following moving in, only that Dorothy was grumpy and we had to eat in the kitchen she controlled. Meals were served at very early times in the nursing home and were made for people who had little ability to chew food. The people who worked in the nursing home were nice women who had to work, not making much of a wage. I saw many of them more than I saw my own family members. Our family congregated in the cabin in the evenings. There we were lulled by the TV and sat together in the smoke-filled room. Mom and Dad smoked so much that the air was like a constant cloud. At a certain time each night, usually late, Patty and I had to take off for the attic. We each were moved into our own rooms. Dad found beds, dressers, and wardrobes. I had never had my own room before. If I wanted a private place, I used to hide in the big closet, very quietly. It was nice to have my own private place—a place to get away from everyone else, a place I could shut the world out, and a place where I could pray openly and freely, without fear of anyone catching me or making fun of me.

There was one positive thing that accompanied the move from Chicago to the nursing home. We would be living in a small town and I would be able to find a church that I wanted to attend. And I would be free to go. I vividly remember when Dad was telling us what the town was like. I became very bold and told him I wanted to find a church to go to. He did not resist, but said I could. I was excited and worked with Mom on my plan to find a church, all on my own at the age of eight.

My first room in the attic was haunted. I would awake in the night with doors banging and boards creaking. There was a little door in each room that led into a small, unfinished storage area. This door would sometimes fall open during the night. Nightmares started, and I had to sleep with my light on. I finally moved my mattress out into the hallway, away from all of the strange and spooky feelings I had when I was in that room. Of course I did try to tell my parents, but they attributed everything to just bad dreams. After a couple of years, I finally conned my sister into changing rooms with me. The room she had faced the front of the house and had a much warmer feel to it; it was almost cottage-like. I was never afraid in this room nor experienced the strange phenomena that happened in the other room. Besides, Patty did not care where she slept, because she was never there. It did not take her long to make a best friend at school. Every night Patty would sneak out of the nursing home and spend the night with her friend. This made the attic all the more foreboding to me, knowing I was really on my own. I don't know how Patty got away with it all those years, sneaking out, but she did. I don't know what time or when she came back. It was not until she was in junior high that Mom paid any attention to what she did. Somehow she found out Patty had a boyfriend. I think one of the ladies that worked in the nursing home told her. After she found this out, after Dad went to bed, Mom would come up to the attic, drag me out of bed, and down the street to spy on Patty and her friend. Of course, Dad never did find this out or his rage would have been uncontrollable. Patty and Mom had fights about this. But Patty never listened to anyone. She still went out and about and did whatever she wanted.

After I learned that Patty was never around at night, and it took awhile for me to realize this, my nighttimes in the attic became even more fear-ridden. I really was alone. Not understanding what was wrong with Dorothy, what her mental state was, and what she would or would not do became another torment to me. If we were too noisy, she would angrily come out and say something. When I was alone in the attic, I felt unsafe, wondering if she would come out of her room and do something drastic, like things I had seen in horror movies. There was no one I could talk to about anything, not even this.

Meals in the nursing home became something that I tried to be late for, a pattern of course already established by the time I was in first grade. By the time I awoke in the mornings, breakfast was over. I found Wheaties and Cheerios in the walk-in pantry every morning and could stand in the pantry, hiding, eating these to my heart's content. However, these were not just for breakfast. These became my best friends and the main courses for many of my meals over the next four-year period. I also drank copious amounts of milk like a parched dessert straggler would take to water. Dorothy did not talk but continuously grumbled under her breath. She and the ladies who worked in the nursing home would glare at me as I took the milk and hid in the pantry to drink it with my cereal. Sometimes I would walk out to the back porch to be beyond their range. They made remarks loud enough for me to know their disapproval. At lunch and dinnertime, the patients were fed first, then the employees, and last, us. Usually there was nothing left, and I mean literally nothing except the scrapings of gooey bread pudding. When I came home from school for lunchtime, everyone was finished eating by then. Only Dorothy was left in the kitchen. I would hide in the pantry, standing up, stuffing the Wheaties or Cheerios and milk into my mouth as fast as I could swallow. At nighttime, it was much the same, what was left was unpalatable. My routine became constant. When I had my own children, they were six and four before I ever bought them any prepackaged cereal—and only then because they cried and felt deprived because they were not eating what their friends ate and what they saw on TV.

There was one meal that I loved, and that was Sunday dinner. Dad was a great cook—he had been a cook in the Army during World War II—and he cooked the Sunday dinner, so there was always plenty for all of us, too. He made wonderful homemade pies and fried chicken with mashed potatoes and gravy. I loved these meals, and he did this for years, well into my high school years. I would stuff myself until I could hardly walk. Of course, Patty was not around. I don't know where she ate. I'm assuming at her friend's. Mom was usually in the nursing home somewhere working. I don't know what happened to Jimmy. I think he just did not eat—maybe Mom took a plate to him in the cabin. I don't remember any more. He had gotten into the pattern of eating only hamburgers while we still lived in Chicago, so if Mom came in every day and made him his hamburger he would eat. If she didn't, I don't know what he did. He just was so skinny, and of course, this was the time when his not growing really began to show, between the ages of six and twelve.

I remember many nights being in the sitting room of the nursing home in one of the big stuffed plastic rockers—rocking, rocking, and rocking. Not even really watching the TV programs, but lulling myself, until I was finally drowsy to a point when I thought I could sleep. The night woman frequently had to shoo me off upstairs, late, often after ten or eleven. Once upstairs, my sleep patterns were in turmoil. I would sneak carefully down the stairs with my comforting quilt and pillow in hand, cautiously stepping to not make the stairs creak, and then cringing and stopping when they did. My destination was to sit in the big front porch swing, hopefully to be able to settle into a peaceful sleep. I would be there no matter what the weather was, summer, winter, rain, or snow. I found my way there, to the fresh air, outside of the nursing home, with no in-house sounds, only the sounds of outside nature, especially that of the wind in the treetops. I would curl up in my blanket, cuddle to my pillow, and push the swing, back and forth, back and forth, becoming drowsy, finally into sleep. Oftentimes I would swing so hard, I would bang the front wall of the house. After so many bangs, I would get a scolding from the night lady. It did not matter to me. This was the only place I could find peace. It was my refuge. And when the hearse would come to pick someone up during the night, I would grab my things and hide around the north side of the house, away from the streetlights and under the fire escape stairs. I would stand and wait, wanting so badly to sleep, until the body was taken, the hustle was over. Then I would settle back into the rhythmic swinging. I blocked out of my mind what I had just seen, not fully comprehending the magnitude of the events surrounding me and totally unable to encompass what death meant.

The nursing home, in the days of the fifties and sixties, was a place where people were put who could not care for themselves any longer. Many were bed ridden, or just moved from bed to chair. Some could walk slowly up and down the hallways to the bathroom. Their days must have been long, with nothing to look forward to but another day just like the one before. Watching these people put a powerful drive within me that I never wanted to grow old, I never wanted to stop living, and I never wanted to let the futility of this life have power over me.

Around the nursing home, no one ever really talked about death, or after life, or grieving. The discussions in the morning centered around who had died or who had come close to death the night before. It was always unpleasant to walk into the kitchen in the mornings. As hard as I tried to blot out what I heard, I still heard. My gut would wretch inside. I escaped out the back door as fast as I could. As I heard the people around me speak so easily and callously of these things, or not speak of them, I unconsciously learned it was something to keep hidden, not faced. I did not know nor understand why. It just all became mysterious, along with all of the other unspoken things that became entombed around my being.

The memories of the nursing home obviously forged a huge impact on and in my life. The first was the residents. We called them patients back then. Old people love little children. They love to grab them and try to talk to them. My parents encouraged me to talk to the residents in the nursing home. After several encounters, they became something that all of my meanderings and steps were to avoid. They would love to grab me and pull me over to them and try to talk to me or hug me. I will never forget the feel of their skin and flesh, the look in their eyes of longing for life and love, the desperateness in their voices for someone to talk to them and notice that they were there. I longed to avoid these encounters, being nauseated by the odors and feel of their skin, but mostly wanting to hold back on the life force I felt they were seeking from me. It was grueling, to feel them tug, to want that life force, and to feel the energy flow out of my own body. I had to become almost like a stone, rolling through, with no emotions, with no stopping, just rolling through. I learned to hide all of my emotions, fears, and questions on a much deeper level than what I had to learn to survive within my family. Things were shoved off in my head, like they did not exist.

Many children have a keen spiritual sensitivity. It is natural to them up to a certain age. I was one of those who had this sensitivity. When death was close for a person, I became lethargic, often lingering for hours in one of the plastic rocking chairs, knowing another person was being enclosed and encompassed by this mysterious rite of passage. I would feel the despair of it. I would walk by the rooms where death was lurking on my way to bed or the bathroom. I could feel death in those rooms, waiting for its victims. Sometimes I could sense the reactions of the victims by their breathing, by their cries, by the words they would speak out. I ached inside for the suffering and agony that had become their lives and for the way in which it all had to end.

I have vivid memories of three people as they became death's victims. One was a woman who had never been married and had a private room. I never saw her the whole time I lived there. She stayed in her room. The sense that she welcomed death and wanted to be in another existence pervaded her room and outside of her door. She quietly gave way to the shallow breathing, with no fighting, no groaning, and no cries. There was a glow in her room along with the feeling of peace. Now as an adult I know this was the presence of angels waiting to help her on to the other side. The second is of another woman who was in a room with two other women. She was anxious, not fearful, but anxious. I could sense resistance, quiet resistance. She took days to go and I felt such compassion at her quiet suffering. The third was Mr. Jones. Mr. Jones was in the parlor room with the grand fireplace, right off the sitting room. He had also been days in this process. I don't remember if he had a family, but they weren't there at the time he needed them. Most families were not there at these times, in those days. So, the only person left for him became my dad. Mr. Jones had become horribly hysterical and the ladies who worked in the nursing home could not control him. It became obvious around nine o'clock on a certain night that he would not make it through the night. I sat in the big overstuffed rocker, rocking away, listening to his cries and his agonizing questions. He would yell and scream at the top of his voice, a voice that rang throughout the whole nursing home, and a voice that no one could refrain from hearing. Mr. Jones insisted that my dad tell him that there was life after death, that death was not his end. He kept begging and begging and begging for Dad to tell him. Dad sat there, quietly by his side, his face set to not show any inward emotions. Finally after much begging by Mr. Jones, around eleven at night, I faintly heard my dad say, "Yes, there is more, this is not the end." Mr. Jones relaxed. I went to bed in the attic. The hearse came about two in the morning. Mr. Jones bequeathed his only possession that he had in the nursing home, an old brown radio, to my dad. Dad kept that radio for over twenty-five years, until they retired from the nursing home business. I remember my thoughts sitting in the chair listening to the agonizing cries of Mr. Jones, longing for faith in something he did not know. I thought how ironic it was that my dad had to be the one to comfort him. Mr. Jones did not know my dad was not only an unbeliever, he was an antagonistic unbeliever. But Mr. Jones never knew that. I knew this was a good deed my dad had done.

My first personal encounter with death was when I was six. We were living in Chicago in Aunt Martha's basement. Early one Sunday morning I was the only one up, as I often was sitting up in the living room at all hours of the night or early morning since I had so much trouble sleeping. Therefore, I was the one that answered an unexpected knock at the door. It was Aunt Martha holding our wonderful kitten, Tuffie, who was about three months old. She held Tuffie upside down by all four legs. "Look at what happens when you don't take care of your kitties," she screamed at me. I looked at the little lifeless cold body, as she laid her on the floor. I remembered the life, the love, and the fun in this kitty. He brought much delight into our lives by his silly antics. Later Mom said she was blaming me because it was her drunken boyfriend that ran Tuffie over. It could not erase the sense of guilt that somehow I was to blame for this. It carried through my whole life, reinforcing the feeling that somehow I was responsible for everything bad that happened or could happen.

Encountering death in a strange home, with these older people I did not know, and in such traumatic circumstances became experiences that I became numb to. I was probably trying to not take the experiences into myself, but actually did so. How could a child know any different? My sanctuary and salvation became nature, finding release and love in nature, both the plant and animal kingdoms. I had more pets than Carter had little liver pills (only the older generations can relate to this analogy). Pets ranging from fish, turtles, frogs, toads, hamsters, mice, cats, and on and on, any kind of small animal I could beg my parents into letting me keep. No dogs though, Dad had the dog. These little animals became the delight of my life, my focal point of escape from the surroundings. When they would die, I would hold services for them in the burial section of what I ironically called my "garden plot" and never dig in that spot again. The soil in my "garden plot" was so dead it would not even grow weeds. I wanted to create some beauty in my life, something that would make me feel alive on the inside and give me something to smile about on the outside. So every spring I would faithfully plant the seeds, looking at the beautiful picture on the outside of the seed packet, imagining all the while I would hold this beautiful thing in my own hands.

It was in the nursing home that I learned to work—and work then became the avenue of my acceptance by my family and the way that I learned I could earn acceptance and my sense of value for many years into the future. I finally knew Mom valued me for something. Mom was always exhausted by the hard physical labor she did in the nursing home. Since she was the owner, all responsibilities, no matter how big or how small, always fell back onto her. She was always complaining about it. To help comfort her, I asked to help with the laundry in the nursing home. Now in those days, laundry was done in the basement, an old fashioned cemented, unfinished basement. There were two wringer washers and four rinsing tubs. These washers and tubs were filled via hoses attached to faucets in utility sinks. Strong detergents and bleaches were used in all of the cycles, to counteract the strong urine and feces odors and bacteria. There were mounds of laundry to be done daily, since much of the bedding had to be changed daily due to bodily mishaps. Many of the people were in some kind of cloth "diaper." The water in the washers was scalding. We had to use special sticks made from boards to pull the laundry out of the tubs into the wringers, carefully executing the movements to not catch the sticks, our fingers, or arms in the wringers. After rinsing and wringing again, the clothes were put into heavy metal baskets and hauled up the basement stairs to be hung on the outside clotheslines. We had basement clotheslines also, but those were only used on very cold icy days when there was no hope of outside drying. I don't know why Mom had this job, but she did. It weighed heavily on her. At the age of nine, I decided it was my duty to help relieve her of her burden. On Saturdays I would try to do as many loads as I could. The baskets of wet clothes were so heavy. I remember dragging them up the basement stairs, trying to hang everything so perfectly. Mom was so particular about how things were hung, even though she barely bothered to clean our cabin. No matter how perfectly I tried to please her by doing what I thought she said, she would grumble and have to come out and redo what I had done. She was even fanatical about having the socks all hung in the same direction, so the heels were all facing the same way. Not that this made them dry any better, but I learned that to try to please her, these fanatical theatrics became something that was normal. I felt like such a failure. I would run home after school to try to help take down the nursing home laundry, only to see that she had to refold everything after me. I did keep it up though, resenting all the Saturday and after-school time I could not play. Trying so hard to please her overwhelmed my own sense of anything that I could have wanted for myself.

Another responsibility that I took on at the age of eight was becoming the one responsible to clean the cabin, our home. It was hard work because no one ever picked up after themselves. Mom and Dad never emptied the overly large ashtrays, spewing ashes everywhere. Dirty dishes were allowed to pile up. I wanted to let Mom know I cared, so I started cleaning. Instead of it being something that was appreciated, it became something that was expected. I became enslaved to the cleaning up after my family from then until I got married at the age of twenty-one. When I was twelve I took on all the family laundry and ironing. This responsibility fell onto me because I had taken steps to do my own laundry. Instead of appreciation, Mom became angry about why I did not do everyone's. I became the one responsible. These patterns enhanced the strange sense of needing to take care of my dad. Now besides feeling emotionally responsible for him, I had the physical burden of a family. It was a heavy burden to carry for many years. For years, even up into my fifties, I had nightmares of cleaning up after my family. During therapy and after discussing with Miriam the nightmares I would have about cleaning up my family's messes and how exhausted I would be in the mornings, it became obvious, that in these dreams the physical work was the expression of the emotional baggage I took on to soothe and cover over the family pain.

I lived in this nursing home from age eight to twelve. I knew I was different from all the other kids in my class. It was an unspoken sense of knowing something was different, even though I did not feel that different. No friends except for two (one's mother worked at the nursing home) could come to where I lived. I constantly lived in a state of feeling ashamed of living in a home where other parents did not want their children to come. Something that began to make me sense that my life was not normal, was when my friends would tell me what their parents did say about not wanting them to be in the nursing home. I could not understand how I was expected to live in one, but they could not come over for an hour. I felt less. I tried to understand how my parents could let me live in the nursing home, while other children were not even allowed to walk in the doors.

Children's reasoning does not comprehend the reasoning of adults. Every day as I walked by the nursing home, sometimes trying to circumvent it as I found my way to the back door, a deep sense of shame would overwhelm me—the shame of living in something so different, so reproachable by others. I would grieve and scream inside that this place was not me, I could not help it that I had to live here. It did not really matter what I felt—no one cared, no one was there to listen, and I would not have been heard. It was hard for me to face the fact that my parents did not care either, they could let me live in this and they did not even care how it affected me. They probably saw it as taking care of me. I was alone, I felt alone, like a bird of a foreign species dropped in the middle of a strange island, surrounded by no one that spoke the same language. As I said, my salvation was nature and my animals. Another avenue of salvation began to grow. It was my crying out to the Lord to find meaning in all of this. I would take long nature hikes around the edge of town, along the creeks and lake, discovering and loving the little tidbits of nature. I used this as a great avenue of escape from what was waiting for me at home. It also became part of my quest to find the truth of my life. There were days and days of walking through the alleys, along the paths, looking up at the trees and the sky and crying out to whatever my image of God was at the time. What was the meaning of all this—all this internal agony, all the suffering around me, all the sense that there surely was more to life than this?

At the age of twelve, Aunt Jan and her daughter were living in my room in the nursing home. She had left her second husband. I was moved to the hallway. Aunt Jan and

Alice, then six, were subject to all of my belongings. I treasured my belongings. I learned to compensate for everything I did not have by being a collector. I loved to collect animal nick knacks; you could pick them up for a quarter at the dime store. I found many treasures of nature that became keepsakes. I used to store my life in boxes, hide my boxes, and then take things out, string them all around my room to fill up my existence with them, and stuff everything back into the boxes so no one could find them or take them away from me. This became almost a ritual for me. These were treasured times. I always made sure no one was around or I tried to board the door so no one could access my room when I was living in the moment with my treasures. Now Aunt Jan and Alice had my whole life in their control, a life that I could not access without their permission. I was not even allowed to enter my own room without their permission. I would wander around outside at night for hours, not knowing what to do with myself.

Living in boxes, both in the real boxes of my collections and the boxes I created in my mind and feelings around my activities and relationships, became a place of safety for me. It was only recently that I realized this was pretty much how I lived my whole life. Unconsciously I was trying to stay hidden, to keep my life safe and away from where others could invade and take away the things precious to me, even my own person. These inanimate things, these treasures in my boxes, gave me joy and security, things that I loved and I imagined could love me back.

There was one good thing that came out of this invasion of my life by Aunt Jan and Alice. A house came up for sale one block away from the nursing home. I don't know what made Dad even think about it, but I heard him talking to Aunt Jan about buying this house one day. They were standing in the parking lot together. At the mention of a house I sidled up closer to where I could listen. I was holding my breath for Dad to make this momentous decision, praying all the time, "Please, yes! Please, yes!" Dad did not want to spend the money. He really did not like the responsibility of a family or what it took to provide support for a family, denying himself the feeling of being carefree and able to move or go at a moment's notice, even though we had been living in this town now for four years. I had already heard this many times over and over again. Aunt Jan spoke up and told my dad to think what it would mean for the kids. She talked him into buying it. It was awesome, finally a home, our first real home ever. Now I could be like all of the other kids in my class. I was so excited. I could have my friends over.

Now things would change and we would be the "normal" happy American family. I was twelve when Dad bought this house and we lived there until we moved to another small town, to another nursing home that Grandma had left to Dad after she died. Grandma had purchased a different nursing home about ten years earlier and moved to the northern part of the state. We moved to this new town when I was fourteen. This time Grandma left a family home and a nursing home to Dad. So we had a house. I was so thankful. I knew we had a home, like all the other families. I was not ashamed to ask my friends over.

I know many things I experienced over the years were magnified and perceived through the lens of the nursing home experiences. My perceptions are often deeper and beyond what are visibly seen on the outside. Because of this, it has been difficult watching my own body age, watching my own hair turn white, and watching the wrinkles begin. I associated all of these things with old age, which to me meant death. That is what I was surrounded with in my early years. That is what was real to me. Bear in mind that during the 1950s and 60s, our society had a very different, almost secret perspective on "old" people. It has taken me years to accept these natural slowly progressing changes without looking in the mirror and being filled with the terror that the next step for me was to be in that nursing home with death hovering. I've been terrified of aging, of gray hair, or wrinkles, of not having the energy to be physically strong and do things that twenty, thirty, and forty-year-olds can do. Our culture lacks placing the value and respect on elders that is deserved. Being an elder should be the most cherished time in a person's life. We should value the wisdom, the work, and the accomplishments of those who have paved the way for the next generations.

A Short Background
On The Marriage

When I was nineteen, Mom and Dad bought a nursing home in another part of the state, close to where I was attending college. Patty was still living at home. I had stayed out of college for a year during this move. Patty and I worked in a factory and then in a local small restaurant. We spent a lot of time together. I started back to school the next year. Patty got her own friends and I got new friends at school, and our lives started down different paths. I stayed in the dorm during the week but went home most weekends to clean and get everyone's laundry done. Mom was still always so tired from working in the nursing home. Dad had set up his watch repair shop in the basement.

It was during the summer between my second and third year of college that I met my husband. I would work summers at the small restaurant. He was a young local farmer and would come in every evening for his dinner. It took quite a while before we actually started talking to each other. We were both shy. Eventually we went out, and continued to date when I went back to school. It was during the late sixties. Dating and relating then was so different from today. You never really got to know anyone because you were always in the dating-type of mode, putting the best foot forward, being congenial, and, of course, me being nice, which I had learned from the earliest years on. I did really like him and was infatuated with his subtle sense of wisdom. He seemed mature and intelligent. His parents were very upstanding in the community. His grandfather was on the bank board. The family had acquired three farms over the years.

There were times, however, when I wondered why he would say things, where was he coming from. I attributed everything to him being smarter, and, of course, everything was always his way. I did not know any other way to live. Waiting sometimes for hours for him to show up became a way of life, as he was so poor at managing his work respon-sibilities. Instead of questioning this behavior as something I would want included in my life, I became glad just for the fact that he did show up. Our relationship was on his terms. If I had known what my terms would have been and would have spoken them, there would have been no relationship. And it did take years for me to learn that I had a right to have input on matters that involved my life.

We were married the summer between my third and final year of college. We had the standard "church" wedding. I moved into the old large farmhouse that my husband lived in. I had grown up in cities and towns. I had no idea what farm life would be like or bring into my life. I also had no idea what marriage was or what I was getting into. Everyone thought my husband was the greatest. There would be hours when we were dating that he would have to stop back at the farm to finish up work and chores that he did not get around to doing before he would come for our dates. I would wait patiently, unaware of what the circumstances were showing me. I was very naïve and also taught not to question or make waves. I do remember one very cold snowy night in late win-ter sitting in his car in the driveway waiting again for him to finish up something he had not done. It was late and he had picked me up at school and was taking me to my parents. As I sat in the car, looking at that cold winter sky aglow with masses of bright stars, I had a fleeting thought of what this life would be like. As I contemplated my choices, I knew I did not have the courage to disappoint my parents or him in ending this relationship. My parents and sister thought he was the greatest. The memory of this feeling quickly faded away and I had no recollection of it until the year we were getting divorced.

I had the big church wedding more for my mom and sister than for me. I really did not care, but they took to the idea and the planning. I seemed to just be there as things progressed. We had no honeymoon. We went immediately to the farm. The next day he bought me my first pair of rubber wading boots to wear out into the manure of the barnyard lots to help him work. I still did not see what was coming. It did take me years to figure all of this out. The third day after our marriage we were in the hog lot and he got upset because I did not know how to sort out a hog he wanted to take to town to sell. He went into a tantrum, something that I had never seen an adult do before. I was stunned not only at the gyrations and contortions that he threw his body into, but at the words that were hurled from his mouth. With not so much as a goodbye, he jumped into his pickup and was gone to town, leaving me standing in the middle of the lot, smelling of manure, and bewildered. I had just seen the first of many years of this transformative behavior, always transfixing its accusations and condemnations to make me the cause of all of his problems. No matter what the problem or issue was, I was always at fault. As this behavior became more extreme over time, I felt completely trapped in a situation I did not know how to nor have the intestinal fortitude to resolve.

Our first son was born almost two years after we were married. After this, life was really different. I had to begin working long and harder hours on the farm, filling in more and more for the lack of what my husband could accomplish. Life became hard. Money was scarce. Our second son was born two years after the first son. These two young men became my reason for living. They became the focal point of my perseverance through all the years of hardship and abuse. I tried as hard as I could to protect them not only from the unreasonable ravishes of my husband's tantrums and hurls, but from his family who would have liked to have raised them for themselves.

Years after I was divorced, I was praying while working at my kitchen sink and working internally on another level of forgiving my husband and myself for the situation we created in that marriage. I had done this many times before, but knew that somewhere I was still not free inside—there was still some link that had to be removed, cleansed and uprooted. And one day I sensed that because the repentance had finally gone deep enough, was sincere enough, something changed. I remembered the reason why I married him. I remembered the sweet and funny guy that was endearing to be with, the one I fell in love with—the face he usually showed to others, but not to me after we were married. Everyone makes choices every day of their lives. I don't know what motivated my husband to make the choices that changed him into the kind of person he became.

Part Four

THE AFTERMATH OF THE MARRIAGE

How often does it happen, I wonder? You meet someone you think is wonderful to you, fall in love, and want to be with that person. Then after the honeymoon, you wonder who *did* you marry, is this really the person that spoke those vows? For sixteen long years I lived in such a damaging relationship that by the time I finally got out, I did not even know what color I liked or what kind of music I liked to listen to. To go into all of the details of those sixteen years here is not the purpose of this story. However, it is to give a glimpse of moving on, of the rebuilding of a life that had been destroyed by cruelty and fear, to show that we do not need to remain the victims of circumstances that our lives somehow become entangled in, no matter for how long.

There is one time that I think is worth sharing, to illustrate that our lives do mean more than what we are really aware of. There was a time when my boys were early grade school age that I was beyond despair. I was suicidal. That seemed to be the only way out of the daily hatred, verbal abuse, and endless hours of hard labor, from looking for wood to start a warm fire for the boys in the morning, to dragging several hundred feet of frozen hose across hundreds of feet of frozen ground to try to water livestock so I would not be blamed again for the financial disasters that were everyday occurrences in our farming practice. Suicide is no answer for anyone. When in such a mental and emotional state that there is no rational thinking process, consequences are not taken into account. I got the idea this was the only answer. The evening before I had planned to end my life, I received a phone call from Aunt Ruth. She had to call my sister to get my phone number and the first words she said were, "Linda, this is your Aunt Ruth. I don't know why I'm calling you. I guess I have not talked to you in about ten years, but I feel very compelled just to tell you that God does answer prayers." And with this came the realization that this is not the answer, God will make a way, and He did but it did take time. But through that time, He gave me the grace and courage to go on. I saw in this phone call how important each soul is and that we can make it through any circumstance, if we continue to persevere. When it came down to it, I have to believe I would not have ended my life, I would hope not anyway. Thank God, I did not have to find out. I know that no matter how bleak life may seem at the moment, our minds don't always perceive the truth. He is faithful and that is what we hang on to.

After the divorce, getting my life back together did not happen overnight. I had never really been out in the work force to know what it was all about. I lived my life to please others, to take care of their whims so they would accept me. My life went down a path that changed from the all-American dream of falling in love, and living happily after, to a life of fear, torment, and withdrawal from everything that makes our lives loving, fun, and worthwhile. The motivation for staying in a damaging marriage, undoubtedly, was fear, extreme fear that bordered on the edge of terror. When I finally did try to leave, the threat of taking my children away continued to hold me into the bondage of the relationship. One day, however, it did happen, I waited him out long enough, and he gave up. After sixteen years of a life that I never imagined anyone in this country could have lived, I became free.

Free for what? As a young person, I was very skilled in many areas and did quite well in school. My career could have gone many directions. I loved to learn, which helped. But when I got divorced, the young woman who was out to become a psychologist to help provide understanding and healing for others who live with emotional inflictions and suffering became a victim of suffering which I had no idea existed. Living for all those years to the unreasonable rampages, expectations, put-downs, and insinuations of how inadequate I was had made me into someone that not even I knew. I did not know where to go or how to regain a sense of self, a self that was never allowed to develop even before I was married. I could not talk without extreme self-consciousness and fear of making everyone that I did talk to mad at me. I would worry for days about the consequences that might come back after what I said. I had worked long hard hours on the farm, doing chores and labor that was meant for men. How many times over the years I thought that my husband should have had a hired man instead of marrying. He seemed to resent everything about women, perhaps due to his own resentment of his mother, maybe it was transferred to all women. It had the impact and full forceful blows on me to strip me of what little I did still have in life to be joyful about. As time progressed in the marriage, I was not allowed to buy clothes unless they were the cheapest thing on the sale table and marked down many times over. I wore his. Luckily his mother was a master seamstress and loved to make clothes for my sister-in-law and me. For my husband, even this was a luxury. When I needed shoes, we found men's shoes on sale for five dollars. Any sense of being a woman was washed further and further away, replaced with more shame and self-condemnation. Even ten years into the marriage it was still held up to me the fact that he had paid for two ten-dollar dresses the first year we were married, why couldn't I wear them? For a short time I worked for Mom in the nursing home and I had treated myself to a five-dollar bottle of perfume. When he found out he was not only enraged, but accused me of buying it so I would be more attractive to another man. Another man, what a joke, there was no time or energy left in my life to even think beyond the next meal I was to prepare for my family.

What was I going to do, now that I was *free*? I had children to support, and had to start my own home. I had such low self-esteem. Twice, when I was married, I had tried to go back to school, once to finish my degree, and once to get secretarial and computer training so I could get a decent job. He pounded into my head that I could not do anything and that I would fail. I gave up. The consequences were too great. I was also an emotional wreck. The longest period of time I could go without stopping and breaking down into weeping was about three hours, every day. This went on for almost a year after separating. What kind of a job could I hold? I could not be around people because I cried too much, trying to be rid of the deep grief, anger, loss, and sense of bewilderment.

I had the opportunity to start my life anew. Even though I was carrying much baggage with me, I was thankful for the fact that I was alive and I could wake up every morning. I began to look forward to see the sunrise, and hear the birds singing, again. I began to have a weak hope of what my life could become. Divorce meant not having someone around to make me feel like I was not worth anything, like I was a slave to the demands another person's hatreds and insecurities could inflict. I liked being able to listen to any music I wanted to, whenever I wanted without being ridiculed. It did take me a long time to get over the guilt and condemnation when I did do the things that I enjoyed. I liked feeling like I was a person, even a woman, who could express herself by being able to buy a soft feminine dress, or a lacy colorful bra, if I wanted to. The first time I did buy a lacy bra after I became free, I was so riddled with guilt and fear, I became ill. I liked being able to talk to my friends on the phone without having to report back everything I said and without the fear of saying something he would get mad at me for. And sometimes I liked just being able to do absolutely nothing at all.

I started my "career" boom by cleaning houses. A friend in my church cleaned houses for her occupation. The money was very good, plus setting your own hours. This proved very good for the emotional state I was in. Since my physical stamina was not that strong, I could work at my own pace, and stop to rest and eat as I needed to. And I could sit for a spell to do the weeping with no one around to see or hear. There was also another upside to this. I loved to clean. For some unknown reason as a child I loved to clean. I often would go over to one of my girlfriend's houses, and we would clean. She was forced with this responsibility due to a large family and the hours her parents worked. I helped her and it was a delight for me. When my parents owned the nursing home, I took on the role of cleaning our own home. Cleaning became challenging for me and rewarding because I could look back and see what I had accomplished.

I started my own cleaning business, "Fresh As A Daisy" I called it. I delighted in doing special things for people in their homes, cleaning special little places that no one else ever did, under the sinks, doing the windows they looked out from the kitchen or dining areas. Occasionally I would buy flowers for them, a very small bouquet of daisies. I loved watching them look around at how shiny everything looked. They appreciated everything I did. They appreciated me. This was a wonderful feeling in my life, to feel this appreciation so I loved to please them. My self-esteem was still extremely low and has taken years to rebuild. I do remember in the beginning of cleaning the houses, I felt so unworthy. I felt like I should pay the people for letting me come to clean their house.

I had plans to make this into something big. I had plans to make a lot of money for what I wanted to provide for my children, to make up for what they had been deprived of. After one year and the beginning of healing from the marriage, I had just started making real plans and see where I could go by expanding this business. I had no trouble getting new clients. This dream was over quickly. One day while cleaning, I bent over, and something excruciatingly painful happened in my lower back. I was never a person to let any physical pain or illness stop me. I couldn't. I had had lots of physical pain in my body over the years. I had had much illness as a child. On the farm, just the extreme heavy work took its toll. This pain was intolerable, childbirth was a breeze compared to this. For one month I could hardly get out of bed. When this first happened to me, and the doctor told me I would be down for one month, I said to myself, "Nothing can stop me. I won't stay down." Well, I tried to work. I tried to keep going. The doctor was right; it was one month. Luckily, I had my youngest son still with me, and many friends who came to help take care of me.

Treatment was expensive and frequent, in the beginning almost daily. I had not gotten my finances yet where I had insurance, and insurance didn't cover chiropractors at the time. I went to my medical doctor and chiropractors. It was hard going back to cleaning. I worked slowly, often times crawling, to keep the strain off of the injured back muscles. I knew I could not keep doing the housecleaning, even though I really wanted to. I tried to get help from welfare but earned "too much money" for them to help me. My family was not available to help. My mother had died. My dad had fallen to pieces after her death and continued to live from relative to relative for a period of time. My sister and I were estranged at this time due to her and Dad's strong reactions to my spiritual beliefs, beliefs that allowed me to finally have the courage to be a person and speak what I felt in my own heart.

I needed to find something new to do, to try to change directions. One day I had a thought in my mind to take computer classes. Since I had not typed since high school and did not want to come up with the money to take the classes, I put this thought off. One night after a church service, as I walked out of the sanctuary, our three pastors were talking and called me over to them. "Linda, we think you should check into changing your work, maybe look into doing something with computers!" Needless to say, I began to change directions. I took a typing and beginning computer class. I did love the secretarial work. In fact, when I was in high school I had wanted to take the whole schedule of office classes but Dad wanted me to go to college, so I had to take the college prep classes. My dad took a lot of pride in the grades that I got, more pride than he did in me as a person. I had to go to college to please my dad, to make him feel good about himself. Even though I had wanted to be a psychologist, my motivation for going was to please him and I had no drive to do well or succeed for myself.

I worked away at my typing. I borrowed a friend's typewriter—the old manual kind, not electric and certainly not one that typed with the ease of a computer keyboard. I started drilling away to build up accuracy and speed. I loved the computer class. Computers intrigued me. I could pick it up quickly. With my newly acquired skill, I began a job search. Within one week I had two job offers. One was a data entry position for a national testing company. A friend of mine did the same work and we could have ridden together. The second was from the lady that taught me the computer class. She called and offered me the position of office manager and class coordinator. Of course I took the second offer even though I knew I could not do it, having neither the experience nor training. Pat was the owner of this business that provided resumes, business communications, computer and office skills classes, and career counseling. Pat had faith in my abilities. After she and I became friends, she told me how it came about that she called me. She was sitting in her office one day, knowing that she needed someone who could function a specific way. She had many employees who were part time and did not stay long. She sat at her desk with a pile of resumes in front of her and asked in prayer who could do the job she needed. She said my face came into her mind and the town where I lived. She went through all the files of classes she had taught within the last year to find my phone number and name. When I started, I did not even know how to address a business envelope on the typewriter. She taught me everything. Everything I had wanted to be since high school, that professional secretary, came into existence for me. That and more—I learned how to interview professionals and write resumes; how to research, develop, and teach classes; how to manage an office and work with employees. Pat had been in business for twenty years and I learned from watching and listening to her. I spent many hours on my own time studying and fine-tuning the abilities and knowledge I needed to help her business grow. Plus we became very good friends.

The next job I went to was also a stretch for me. I was hired into a national manufacturing facility. This is where I met Adam, but that was years down the road yet. Again, it was a time of learning, growing, developing my skills, mostly on my own time and initiative to do the kind of job that I wanted to be known for. The experience I gained from working within a manufacturing facility with eight hundred employees was an education within itself, especially in relating to all kinds and types of people. I was moved into positions at a moment's notice. I had six different positions over eleven years. The skills and knowledge I developed to do these jobs have served my employment opportunities quite well. The thing was, no one knew how hard I had to work to make these jobs happen. Plus, no one knew where I had come from, from crawling to clean someone's house to training hourly personnel to create statistical reports for corporate meetings. I loved this work. The relationships with the other employees were fun and fulfilling. I was friend to both the hourly and the salaried. One night while out with one of my hourly friends, she made a comment to me about how I had it made. She was looking at my job and what I did, thinking all of this was handed on a silver platter. Neither she, nor others, saw how much I worked behind the scene to make all of this happen, to make all of this successful for the facility. This was an interesting revelation to me, again, how she saw me, through her eyes, feeling like she was stuck in her production job. All the while I knew if she tried and worked hard, she could move on. There were other hourly personnel, however, that I worked with that did move on into administrative and professional roles. I loved being able to help people realize that many of the limitations we think we have are only because we think we have them. I felt I was living proof of this principle.

Of course, the plant is where I met Adam, and the whole inside of me began to churn upside down. I was still there when I had the car accident. I did move on, however. I went to work in a university setting and my learning process started all over again. It was at this new job that my love for working with the written word had an opportunity for expression. I worked with proposals, letters, and various procedures and communications that allowed me to expand my writing and editing talents even further.

At the completion of the writing of this book in 2006, I believe I'm ready for the greatest things yet to come in my life. In my "spare" time I have spent the last nine years researching and learning the publishing business. I have three series of children's books planned and anticipate sharing them with the world. I also would like to turn what I have learned into an avenue to help others in the telling of their stories, to help others who have something to say. I have learned this one simple truth: never give up, find within yourself the desire and drive to be and express everything that is in your being to be. This may mean going back and getting in touch with someone that is buried within you, that young child that had hopes, visions, interests that may have been squelched or squandered through the years. It may mean getting a new relationship, going back to school, changing where you live. Whatever it is for you, find it and do it. Give it time—it takes faith, steps, determination, and perseverance. It is time for all of us to see ourselves through hope, through eyes that see us as everything we are meant to be. It is time for healing and wholeness—on the inside of our beings—so the outside expresses who we really are.

MY SPIRITUAL QUEST

We live in the land of the free, in a country that was founded and built by its forefathers on the basis of spiritual freedom, that each person can worship the Lord in their own way. Yet, I was five before I was "allowed" to go to church. This became a pattern of my spiritual quest throughout my life, wanting to find more of Him, being misunderstood and criticized not only by my family, but other believers who wanted to keep my beliefs and experiences within the confines of what theirs were. It has seemed I was always rocking the boat of other's belief systems.

"Wait! It can't be over yet. I can't go, I haven't seen God yet!" Mom had me by the hand and was tugging me through the massive crowd of the large Gothic-style Lutheran Church in the heart of Chicago. We must have walked a mile to get there. "Come on, Linda, will you just come on," Mom grumbled as she jerked my arm and tried to hurry out of the crowd, on toward home for her to get dinner. Patty was in front of her, held by Mom's other hand, with the same disinterest and wanting to get out of the crowd that Mom exuded. I paid no heed to either of their taunting as my five-year-old body and face agonizingly stretched up toward each person that I brushed by, and then the person next to them and on and on, longing to get a glimpse of God's face. My heart sank as we left the crowd, and I asked Mom, "Where was God, I did not get to see Him."

We had been planning to go to church for a whole month,

maybe more. I was five years old. It took this long for Dad to agree to let Mom take us kids to church. "But you can't take Jimmy, a son of mine will never believe in God," Dad bellowed at her as she crouched and slunk away into the kitchen to avoid more confrontation. I was ecstatic at the thought of finally getting to go to church, I had been asking ever since I could remember. And now, yes, it was going to happen. In preparation for our event Mom kept saying, "You will get to go where God is." The expectation and anticipation were overwhelming for me, even better than waiting for Santa Claus. It was the first time I had been in a church that I could remember. The crowd was massive, and I felt swarmed over and smothered by the tallness of everyone, unable to see up or outward. As I sat in the pew, listening, I knew I had to see God's face, see Him who talked to my heart and gave me courage to live through each day.

When we arrived home, Dad had already been hitting the bottle and his speech was slurred. "So, did you see God?" He directed this toward Mom. And on and on he went as her shoulders and head slumped low as she moved about the kitchen preparing the meal. Patty and Jimmy ran outside to play; it was a bright spring day. I sat in the "discipline" chair, the chair that he used to punish me in when I would try to talk and he did not like to hear what I had to say. The chair was right inside the living room doorway that adjoined the kitchen. I listened as he ridiculed and cajoled, the antagonism and bitterness booming throughout the apartment. I sat and listened, feeling sickened deep inside of my being. My joy of finally being able to go to church was replaced with fear—fear of letting out how I really felt and believed so that I could escape the harsh verbal thrashing.

Actually though, I had experienced this "god" thrashing myself, many times, until I finally learned to keep my mouth shut, causing me to live for almost fifty years feeling a sense of failure and shame that I could not defend the One that I knew loved me, who had made Himself real to me. After my initial experience with the Lord at three, something else changed in my life. Perhaps this had always been, but I was never aware. Dad became almost violent when he would drink, focusing that violence in vehement words about God. And it was probably about this same time that Mom began to talk to us kids about God. Now it was interesting to me that she wanted us to know that God existed, but she never had the courage to talk back to my dad when he would go on his rampages. By the time I was four I remember listening to him, usually every Saturday night when he was drinking, and wanting to shut him up. I began to speak up and say there is a God. Dad was a brilliant man with a photographic mind. He asked me to prove it. And he would go on and on about the Crusades, about churches, about all of the things that people did in the name of "god" that were harmful to people, even brutal. The worst thing about this though was the loud voice, the look in his eyes, the deep anger, and the feeling of personal attack toward me. Mom used to try to tell me to be quiet, not wanting to cause him to continue on, accelerating his intensity. I don't know how long of a period of time I tried to argue the point with him. But how could I, I had no proof of evidence, no wisdom of book knowledge. I was only four years old. I only had the experience of remembering Him, of that feeling living within my heart, and of hearing that voice daily as my life endured.

Unable to voice or defend what I knew, I withdrew my beliefs into myself, probably what Mom had to do years earlier. But with that withdrawing, I harbored a deep and knowing sense of failure and guilt about living in a situation where the name of the Lord was being put to shame, ridiculed, and taunted. It affected my own sense of worth. It has been in the writing of this book that this sense of failure, of feeling like I had to choose God or Dad, and the anxiety that resulted, have been relieved and put to rest.

It wasn't just the word thrashings about God that taught me silence as survival. It became Dad's way to want to continually criticize me, to attack the way that I thought, to attack how I interpreted living. While very young, I had a sense that I had a right to speak and if it disagreed with his perspective, I still had that right. His demeanor had beaten this out of me by the time I was nine. His most famous phrase to me was, "Linda, you should be ashamed for thinking that way, or for saying that." Shame piled upon shame. Physical and emotional shame was now compounded by the shame of my own thoughts and feelings of how I felt about my life and everything around me. I learned that I had no right to express anything personal, not even a feeling.

It is natural for children, young children under the age of five, to be very in touch with their spiritual side. I know this not only from my own experiences, but also from having children and grandchildren and from working with children in church-related activities. This side is something that begins to have less awareness and influence in our lives as we move out into the "real" world, as we begin to learn, as we begin to be taught that what we see in front of our eyes is truth and reality. Children's angels are very active and children's spirits are often taken up during the night into the heavenly places where they are nurtured and taught. Babies and small children see and experience spiritual things, and as our culture begins to form our thinking processes we lose this. The reasoning power of our minds replaces the openness to the spirit and we become engrossed in only what our physical eyes can see, that becoming the only reality to be aware of, as our lives become a striving to find outward—and inward—fulfillment as we live on.

I remember vividly the feelings I had after my experience with the Lord at the age of three. I stood inside the bed hallway of the trailer. Patty was asleep in her little bed. The bigger bed was empty. I stood there unable to grasp where I was and what I was doing. I looked into the other room, the kitchen, and there were Mom and Dad. I did not understand what they were doing. I don't know how long I stood there, he was groping her and trying to kiss her, and she was teasing him. I did not understand these actions until much later in life. I heard her say, "Get rid of her." Dad looked over and told me to get back to bed. I did not know what to do. I was still so lost in my experience of being with the Father, that as I looked at my bed, I just stood there. I moved slowly back into the doorway. Dad came and picked me up, and tucked me into bed. He did not stay this time. It was shortly after this that Mom changed the sleeping arrangements. Maybe it was an unaware moving of the Spirit that changed the sleeping arrangements. Maybe I really would not be here, if this had gone on longer.

After this experience I had a new dimension added to my life. Prayer. No one taught me how to pray, I just knew after this. I found places to hide where I would get down on my knees and spend long periods of time in prayer talking to God like He was not only my Father, but also my closest friend. When we finally moved out of the trailer into the apartment, then a house, I would hide in the closets. I used to chuckle as I would hear Mom or Patty or Jimmy walking through the place looking for me, but I kept my secret spots. The best spots however were outside in nature where what I was doing was not obvious, quiet spots where I could meditate without disturbance or fear of being caught. I did this for years to come, several times throughout the day. Through grade school and junior high I always began my day opening the bedroom window or peeking out an outside door, early in the morning as the birds were awakening, listening to their songs and letting the love and gratitude within my heart rise in unison with their songs as we awakened with each new day. Then I would jump back into bed, not yet ready to get up, but longing for sleep and the peace that sleep could bring from daily living.

When we moved from Chicago to a small Midwestern town when I was eight, I determined that I would go to church. When Dad was telling us how we would move and what it would be like living in a small town, I was excited. We would be able to walk places on our own, even to "downtown" to where stores were. Living in the area of Chicago that we did, no place was safe. Our playground was the street in front of the house, there were no yards, and our limitations were the one side of the block that we lived on. I had no idea what moving to a smaller town would be like, but I knew I wanted to go to church. Since no one had to walk me there, I could go on my own. Dad agreed. I was determined to try to find avenues to live out what drove me, what was in my heart. When we finally moved, Mom helped me make a plan on how to choose a church. I went about it rather scientifically for an eight-year-old. I had a list of churches that they gave consent for me to attend. Mom talked to the women who worked in the nursing home to get an idea about the churches and I met kids at school that went to the different churches. The Catholic Church and the Pentecostal Church were out. Dad had been raised a Catholic and had been used as an example of a sinner in front of the whole congregation by the priest when he missed church—and these were the times when he stayed with his grandparents, even once when his grandfather was dying.

Small town Midwest is very class oriented. And I found this to be so prevalent in the churches. It was my first real experience with this since living in Chicago everyone seemed to be in a melting pot, the distinction between ethnic groups only beginning to make itself known to me. It was obvious at school which group a child belonged to; they only talked to others in that group. The rules were unspoken but were loud and clear, you only talked to those in the socio-economic class that your parents' level let you achieve. To find "my church home" I tried both church service and Sunday school and attended for several Sundays. I felt very shy and afraid yet also very brave that I got to make this decision about my life. And I was compelled to do so. I would sit in the service and listen to what the minister would say. Sunday school was usually before and I would listen to the "moral" of the lessons that they were trying to teach. The realization of the hypocrisy in all the churches was evident immediately. It made my inside heart hurt to see how the "lower" class kids were treated and snubbed in school, yet while everyone of all classes sat in these Sunday school teachings and services all hearing the same lessons. Disillusionment set in, yet I still had a resolve to belong to a church family. I don't know where that came from, I just had this sense that I needed to belong to a church family. I chose a church that was more focused on social issues and activities because I found it to be less judgmental. I was faithful for years, until the pastor began to seek out my "joining" the church. I did not know or understand what that meant. I tried to talk to Mom about it but she provided no insight and said I had to decide for myself. So, I stopped going. In high school, I would go occasionally with my high school friend, who was Catholic. My dad did not care any longer at this point. My church life then all turned inward, expressed only in internal dialogue with no outward expression of any kind of faith or belief.

It was while living in the attic of the nursing home that my heart began to yearn to see people feel loved. Maybe it was from watching the misery of my own family, watching Jimmy's quiet suffering, listening to the suffering of the people in the nursing home, watching the lack of human engagement by the women who worked in the nursing home, watching my classmates tease and ridicule one another, poke fun at someone for their differences—maybe these things and many more too numerous to remember or mention—that created the stir within me for people to know God's love. I watched as many religious shows on TV as I could, not completely understanding all of them and scared by many of them. I had dreams and visions of speaking to seas of faces, sharing with them how much God loved them, longing for their hearts to feel the warmth, acceptance, and safety of that love.

I did not always believe in Jesus, but I learned to. When I was young, I tried reading the Bible; we only had the King James Version. It made no sense to me, the way the words were set into the sentences. I tried and I tried but I had not yet received the Holy Spirit. Most churches did not even talk about the Holy Spirit in those days, except the Pentecostal. However, I prayed and I did find prayers that others had written, stories, and my own inner feeling of knowing Him that kept me. When I was twelve, I was sitting on my bed reading the King James Version about Jesus' life and resurrection. We had been talking about this in church. I remembered when I was ten and after watching a TV program about Jesus at Easter time, learning about His resurrection, trying to resurrect my baby kitten that had died. I remembered the lies about Santa Claus and the disillusionment and deep disappointment of learning that I was lied to, made to believe in something that was not real. I rationalized in my mind that it was more plausible to believe there could be a Santa than to think someone could resurrect from the dead. When I was in college I took a religion class to satisfy a core requirement. I was married by this time. One of our assignments was to read the book of Matthew. This was the very same book I was reading when I was twelve, when I decided Jesus' resurrection could not have been real. This time, however, something was different. I read with an open mind, I was regularly attending church with my husband, and was active in the church. As I read about Jesus' resurrection this time, a strong and overpowering conviction flowed throughout my being. I knew Jesus was real and that He had indeed been resurrected. I got down on my knees and repented and felt Him, His loving, forgiving, encompassing Spirit, come into my heart.

My life took on something new. My life became led by the Spirit and with this a deep hunger and drive to know more and more of the Lord. I did not want just to know about Him, I wanted to know Him as a personal being in my life. I continually read of others' experiences and talked about things in my church that sometimes just made people look at me. The more I learned the more I wanted to know Him. I ended up finding a new church, with much prayer and discussion with the pastor I was leaving. This new church provided something for me that I had longed for, the feeling like my spirit was home, the church family that I desired since my first church experience when I was five. I still am always reading, searching, seeking, but it has taken me all these years to realize that I don't have to explain myself to anyone, that this is the most important thing in life and I have the right to live that out as to how the Lord is working in me. He works in each of us in His own unique way, "to will and to work for His good pleasure."

When I started in this new church, I was introduced to something new, worship, not just the singing of hymns and songs, but singing and worshipping God in the spirit, from the depth of my heart. It was during these deep times of worship that the Lord began to impress upon me how He looks at our world, at mankind. I felt deep compassion and empathy for the suffering in people's lives, not just physical, but deep emotional pain and suffering that does not show on the outside, that is not visible unless we know how to look deeply into another, through His eyes, not the eyes that the world expects us to live up to. It was the knowing of His deep compassion for our inner suffering that became the catalyst for me to have the courage to be obedient to His voice to tell my story. This became the courage for me to expose my inner being and the shame and contempt of my very existence that has been my bondage.

In my new church I found something else I had longed for my whole life, spiritual mothers and fathers. Over the years the relationships have changed as my life in Him changes and grows. While I was growing up one of the main things I felt deprived of was not having a mother who would teach me about the Lord and teach me His ways. I longed for this. This lack created a deep conviction in my heart growing up that when I had my own children I would teach them to know the Lord, to give them this part of life that brings fulfillment and purpose into living.

As I grew more in the freedom of being who I was, my mom, dad, and sister all had reactions. Remember, I was the quiet one, the one who lived to please everybody else. I began to speak and they did not like it. When Jimmy died, Aunt

Ruth called on the phone and talked to Mom and Dad. They ridiculed her and made fun of her as the religious fanatic of the family. When Mom died, the same thing happened, except that by this time, my family saw me as the religious fanatic to also be ridiculed and made fun of. The week before Mom died, she and Dad were visiting my house. I had a sense that she would soon be gone from this world. And I think she knew. She stayed close by me the whole visit and we talked quietly. One afternoon while we were finishing up lunchtime dishes, she leaned over the counter and looked at me and said, "You know that Patty and Dad make fun of you behind your back because of your religion. But I don't, I wanted you to know I don't." This had been happening for many years and I could always sense it. There were always the comments spoken out in general terms or directed at someone who was not present—comments with a stinging tone that pierced my being. By Mom revealing this to me, I acquired the knowledge I needed to be stronger in the days that followed during a time when Patty was estranged from me for many years. The day after Mom died I could not stop crying, a deep grief welled up and flooded the inside of me. As I sought an answer in prayer, the Lord spoke quietly, "You grieve not for what you have lost, but for what you never had." I was overwhelmed with anger as I watched my dad's behavior during the first three days after Mom died and also confused as to how I should relate to Uncle Ted. "Your dad provided for you and took care of you, your uncle loved you, but I am your Father," these comforting words from the Lord echoed throughout my being as I drifted off to sleep crying the night before Mom's funeral.

Dad died in 1997. He was eighty-five. We never healed our relationship. Patty was always the one that did things for Dad throughout the years after Mom died. Patty called me after the hospital called her. Dad had been driven several hours to a hospital that would accept his insurance. I had planned to drive to the hospital in the morning. Patty drove through the night, arriving around three a.m. That night I called Scott, my overseer, and told him my dad was dying. He asked if he was saved and I said I don't think so. He asked his name, and I said, "Don." He said they would pray for him in the morning. Scott was part of an early-morning prayer group in our church that met daily. The prayer started at seven o'clock. Patty said Dad was restless all through the night, constantly moving and non-communicative. She said at seven in the morning his restlessness became quiet and calm. She said his eyes were open and he was looking straight over his head, like he was watching something. Occasionally he would rub his hands over his eyes. She was convinced that he was seeing things that no one else could see—and Patty never talked this way. She said he had a peace about him as his eyes observed what was above his head. At seven-thirty, the exact time the prayer ended, Dad closed his eyes peacefully and went into a permanent sleep. I believe the prayer brought him into salvation as he transferred from this realm into the real realm. It took me years to come to a resolve of forgiveness toward Dad—not just forgiveness for what he did—but forgiveness that allowed internal healing to come into my life so my life could move forward.

I have experienced many things in my life, but there was a lingering effect that has always seemed to scream louder than all the others. It was a belief system that no one could really ever love me. And perhaps a little deeper than this was the underlying belief that I had no worth as a person. It left me with such an inner gnawing that I ignored and shut out the possibility of any male-female relationship, wanting to keep the sharp sting that could overwhelm my soul and spirit as far away from me as possible. I found I could live like this. Adam coming into my life opened up and reactivated this void. In this book, so much attention has been given to describe the interaction between Adam and me because this and the car accident were the catalysts that forced me to face the truths of my life. Even though I considered myself an overcomer of the many obstacles and oppressions that were part of my life's path, I was afraid I might have to live with this one thing forever, not knowing how to find the answer so I would feel like I was enough, I was enough for myself to feel worthwhile.

One day I was watching Oprah. It was a show about two preschool girls, one who could never be pretty or made up enough and the other who was afraid of being fat and watched her diet and exercised continually. One of the mothers had been bulimic and the other had severe self-esteem issues. Dr. Robin Smith was explaining to the mothers that whatever is part of a woman when a child is born becomes part of that child as it passes through the birth canal. In *The Biology Of Belief* Bruce Lipton says that our belief systems are formed from how our mothers and fathers perceive their world when we are in utero. He also says that no matter what we were born into, we can change our belief systems and how we perceive the world. I would call this believing and seeing ourselves through new eyes. The Bible says the blessings, or sins, from the parents pass down to the child from generation to generation. I imagined myself growing inside of my mother and coming down the birth canal into this world—a world of my mother's hatred for herself, for my dad, and for me because I was part of her. In that flash I realized the truth, her hatred still was overriding how I could see and feel about myself. It was the reason why I believed no one could ever love me for me, that I could never be enough. I felt this lie begin to fade away as I sensed the worth that I longed for my whole life could be attainable.

Our minds determine much of our lives, holding the core of our belief systems from which we act out our destiny. It is not the conscious, but unknowingly to us, the unconscious decisions that become the basis of belief systems that keep us from living out whom we are meant to be. It is only when we see ourselves through His eyes that we find the abilities and capabilities to be our true selves. Paraphrasing Proverbs 23:7, for as you think in your heart, so are you.

As I attended and participated in some of the anonymous meetings, listening to people pour out the depths of their innermost being, to the extent that they allowed themselves to be truthful, my heart would grieve and ache at all of the suffering and the magnitude of how many lives are affected by destructive behaviors, unresolved emotional issues, or spiritual oppressions. It was in listening to these inner cries and facing my own that I realized our belief systems must be fueled by something more than a higher power existing outside of us. We must be driven by something greater than what we can create or generate. All religions and even the twelve step programs teach us that God is the answer. He is. But—He is not an answer out there. He has to be an answer inside, in the core of our being, or the void will be filled by something that drives us to be and express what we are not, and we won't be delivered from the destructive behaviors or the demons within or without. God gave us Jesus Christ to be the answer for this void, His infilling. He is the avenue through which we come to know God as our Father and let Him be personal to us, inside of us. Jesus is the person that God has provided for us to be victors here in this life, in this reality. When we invite Jesus to be Lord, in our inner being over every area of our lives, then His victory becomes our

way. He becomes the source of healing, deliverance, understanding, and resolution. He is the source of my strength—
the inner strength that Miriam recognized in me early on in
our meeting together.

Going from feeling guilty and condemned for existing
to experiencing that it is okay for me to have a life is not as
glamorous as what we have been lead to believe by what we
see in the movies. I still find it shocking to me sometimes,
to my mind, my emotions, and my body, to realize that I
have a right to my own feelings, to enjoy what I like to enjoy,
to have my own thoughts. Sometimes the realization is so
overwhelming that I get riddled with guilt, should-have's,
have-to's, and wanting to fulfill expectations and obligations
to others so I feel acceptable and safe. Knowing I have a
right to be me sometimes seems too big. And with this the
responsibility of being me, of being responsible for everything about me, of answering to no one, except to my God,
can begin to envelope me and make me feel like it's too scary
and too unknowing. Then I remember what it is like to not
be free, and my being begins to balance itself out. I remember the car accident and the overpowering sense of having to
answer for myself; no one else was there to take the conviction of where I had not lived up to the responsibilities of who
I was to be and what I was to do.

I take a deep breath, and decide to go on; to live this
moment, this day, with gratitude and love and know tomorrow can be better. The struggle still comes, but gets less,
and each time the intensity is less. I am winning the war of
whose eyes I view my life through. And I am growing in an
inner joy and calm that I never knew I could have. I am free
to be me—but most important to love me, all of me, spirit,
soul, and body.

Ever since the car accident, when even breathing seemed

hard and burdensome on my body due to all of the soft tissue damage in my chest and back area, the first thing I do in the mornings is listen, take in a breath, and give thanks that I am still breathing. My best buddy, Angel Kitty, jumps on me to be petted or runs over and sits on the stool at the window, looking back at me, waiting for me to join him. It seems he knows he is here to encourage my days. After I raise the blinds, we look out the window at the new day, at the beauty of the grass or snow, trees, maybe the sun and the sky. If it is warm outside, I open the window and we listen to the birds. We look at each other, and I give thanks for all of the abundance of my life.

My story could not end without giving credit to where credit is due. The founder of the church I am in used to say, "No one ever comes to the Lord without someone praying for him or her." When I first heard this, maybe ten or twelve years ago, I was a little disgruntled. I thought of the hard struggle I had to be able to go to church without being criticized, misunderstood. I thought of all the hours of prayer, service, study, and sacrifice that I had put into my life. I pondered on this for weeks and one day the truth came up from my inner being. I'm not sure what made it surface, maybe just the seeking for truth without forming my own opinion. It dawned on me as to who in my life had loved me enough to pray for me, and who also had a relationship with the Lord that they knew the power and importance of such prayer. It was Uncle Ted. In this knowing, I saw myself differently, as special, as loved. Not only did he want to adopt me, not only did he buy me that little rocking chair that was a source of comfort for many years, not only did he take those little snapshots of me that were the only source of pictures of me under the age of three, but he loved me enough to want me to have the most important thing in this life, a living relationship with the living Father.

For my fifty-ninth birthday, I received a wonderful gift from the Lord. I had been in the process of writing the bits and pieces of my life to put this book together for the last nine years. I had much healing, but still felt like something was missing, unsure of what that was but knowing it had to do with the feelings created from all the cursing and neglect throughout my whole lifetime. I wanted to know that I was suppose to be alive, that God had a purpose special for me, that I was not just part of the mass, how could I be relieved of that gnawing guilt, condemnation, and contempt that kept me from enjoying life, always feeling like maybe I'm not doing the right thing. As I awoke on my birthday morning, I said good morning to the Lord as I always did. A vision appeared before me. I was taken back to the time when I was three, that night in the little trailer when God the Father took me up and sat me on His lap, when He began to teach me to know Him, when I first experienced the depth of His love. He held a large picture book. He was showing me my life and what my life would mean to Him. I saw my little face looking at the book then looking at Him—I never smiled, but was extremely serious. I don't remember His face nor did I see it in this vision. I only was aware of the complete, careful love He held for me, careful in the respect that the decisions to choose or not choose to do what I saw in the book were *my* choices to make. My life had come full circle, I reconnected back to the eyes that saw me through the unconditional love, that saw me through the eyes of faith of who I would become, of the delight He had in me living out my life to the fullest in this earth. I felt purpose and value within myself—a wholeness in His Presence. Finally, the last bits of scrambled pieces and parts of my life, my thoughts, feelings, experiences were all pulled together like fitting together the pieces of a puzzle. There were no more holes in the puzzle.

For me to find a life that is not riddled with guilt and condemnation—for buying something that is more expensive than a similar thing sitting next to it because I like it better; for watching a movie in the late afternoon because I need some downtime, when I could be working; to feel like it is okay if I want to do something special for myself—is a life that I never imagined that I could live. And I find I am living it. It is miraculous, and I cannot express enough in words my delight in life, this life before me to live out to the fullest.

May you find peace, joy, and purpose for your life as these words penetrate to let His truth manifest in you. May I, and may you, always remember that every day can be a new beginning, if we so choose. Each day is not a day toward the end of your life—but a new day toward the beginning of what is yet to be.

Jesus, I Accept
I turned my face up toward the sky
My heart did ache, my heart did cry.
To fill this hole within my soul
To have no pain, became my goal.
Upon my knees I found His grace
Within my heart, He took His place.
He let me know His love is true
He made me whole, He made me new.